**HOW TO THRIVE IN**

# THE BURNOUT LADDER

RECLAIM YOUR WORK-LIFE BALANCE AND LEARN
**18 TOOLS** TO BEAT **6 STAGES** OF BURNOUT

# ALAN MUSKETT

ISBN 978-1-0685696 (paperback)

Cover Design by Miblart
Edited by Chloe Robinson
Proofread by Nicola Muskett/Noel Parnell
Book layout by Book Polishers

Publisher: Muskett Consultants Ltd.

If you feel like you're
underrate at work,
don't suffer alone.

Best wishes,

Ken

07398 455826

# CONTENTS

# CHAPTER 1
# INTRODUCTION

## The work pandemic

It is 2 a.m. I wake up, fully alert. There is no transition between sleeping and waking. No bleary-eyed reaching for an alarm, nor taking a couple of minutes to come round. My eyes have flung open and my head has jerked from the pillow as if I have heard the footsteps downstairs of a knife-wielding intruder. Honestly, my mind and body could not be more ready to act if it was. My heart is pounding, and there is no trace of tiredness within me. I know immediately that that's about it for a night's sleep. And now comes the slow, creeping realisation that Monday morning is drawing inexorably closer, and I am just not ready for it. A dull headache from the final glass of escapist red wine last night is starting to announce itself too.

I have a weekly townhall at 9 a.m. and I need to think of something inspirational for the team to hear. If only

I had spent some time during Sunday doing some more prep. I feel guilty for not working over the weekend, and now I am living the consequences which is stressing me out. I will never go back to sleep, even though I crave it. Going into work is merely going to be a survival game on Monday. How do I get out of there without looking like an indecisive, disorganised fool—exposing my leadership failures or simply just drying up and having nothing to say? My mental machinery starts to chew over what I am going to say in the meeting, hashing and re-hashing the agenda. I am already predicting the exasperation of my team, each of whom will have no doubt prepared their questions for me, which I seem ill-equipped to answer. At about 3:15 a.m., I crawl out of bed and go downstairs to fire up my laptop.

I was on the way to burnout. I sort of knew it, but I couldn't seem to avoid it.

According to a mental health report from 2022 by Deloitte UK (Ref. 1), 63% of employees surveyed had experienced at least one of the three symptoms of burnout as defined by the World Health Organization (WHO):

- Emotional exhaustion
- Cynicism related to the job or work
- Reduced professional efficacy

These symptoms sound fairly unpleasant, don't they? But as I will show you, they are much more personally intrusive than that. It is difficult to get truly accurate information on burnout diagnoses, as it is sometimes hard to discern its symptoms from mental illnesses such as depression. Burnout is not new. It has been a scourge of the working world since modern civilisation began. The syndrome, if I can call it that, has been around for millennia, and it was referred to by philosophers in Ancient Greece, yet it is not officially labelled as an illness, but merely a factor influencing health status. It was only introduced officially in the International Classification of Diseases (ICD) in 2019, produced by the WHO (Ref. 2). It is mentioned in the, The Diagnostic and Statistical Manual of Mental Disorders (DSM), used in North America, but not as an official diagnosis (Ref. 3). My guess would be that this will change in the coming years. This is a pandemic, an invader amongst us.

In Deloitte's report, it was estimated that total costs of around £55 billion to the UK economy are due to work-focused psychological problems. The greater part of that figure is down to Presenteeism—that phenomenon where we are at work, but we're really not. We're just going through the motions and faking it, even though, inside, we are dying. People are suffering, yet not taking time off work, probably because they are fearing repercussions, getting fired, or not getting paid. For businesses, huge costs are being incurred and misery is heaped upon individuals and families due to pressure of work as they struggle to balance it with home life. We cannot ignore this, and there is a business case to invest in equipping individuals with the tools to cope. However, while I can understand it is hard to allocate budgets for mental health awareness and training when you can't see tangible benefit to the bottom line, isn't it just fundamentally the right thing to do? Employers have a duty of care obligation to keep their employees safe. Yet, even when funding is set aside with all good intention, it is too easy to slash the spending when sales targets have not been hit and the squeeze on costs takes hold.

## Why I wrote this book

I see anxiety levels climbing through the roof. I also know what it's like to suffer in this way, and I would like to help others either prevent their own burnout path or guide them off it when they are already struggling. Mental health training should be a right for the individual, in the same way that we should be taught how to run a household or manage our finances when we are at school. I get frustrated after talking to companies about the obvious need to help employees look after themselves, only to hear that the plug is pulled on running workshops due to budgetary constraints. Often, the money we are talking about is a drop in their ocean. Individuals' potential improvement in well-being is being held back by financial decisions driven by the need to satisfy shareholders. My business partner and I worked with a company and trained the entire workforce in mental health resilience. It cost them a little over £20,000 on a turnover of just over £100 million. That's 0.02% of their turnover. Nothing. A drop in the bucket. If you doubled it, nobody would bat an eyelid, but the effect on productivity, morale, and health really would move the needle. In the Deloitte report mentioned above, the positive effect of mental health training was calculated at an increased productivity of £4.70 for every £1 spent.

I really succumbed to work stresses in 2013, after taking on a senior management role with a major blue chip food company. I was experiencing burnout, but no doctor ever told me that, partly because I never gave them a chance to do so. I didn't fancy admitting that I was in trouble, and I certainly didn't want to be taking tablets to help me. I was equally afraid of telling anyone at work that I seemed to be struggling with my mental state. I put way too much pressure on myself to be something I could never hope to achieve: the perfect boss and leader. That's how I got into the angsty tangle that I described in the first paragraph. Back then, there was less tolerance of poor mental health as a discussion point, but it's my fault that I didn't say anything, nobody else's. I was just afraid it would look bad on me, and that I would be red-ringed, labelled as someone who couldn't hack it, then replaced by someone who could deal with pressure better than me. Isn't that what keeps most of us chained to our desks, laptops, and machines? The fear of being replaced. The fear of failure.

To help myself, I had to get a grip on my mind and its incessant negative storytelling and catastrophising. My approach to repair my mental state was through mindfulness. I will introduce some useful tools on that topic in this book, and it is a wonderful way of quietening the mind and gaining perspective on thoughts and feelings without hiding from them. I loved it so much that I trained as a meditation teacher so I could share my learning and experience with others. In fact, once I had got myself back together, I could see how much everyone else around me was suffering too. I don't believe there were any long-lasting effects; the experience will have made me stronger and more able to protect myself now. I imagine I have a few more worry lines, and my sleep patterns have never quite been the same, but maybe that's just part of getting older. I think that burnout is like cutting your finger deeply so that a scar forms. The pain does go away, but there will always be a mark, perhaps like craters on the moon. A now-harmless reminder of a more troubled time.

I am not a psychiatrist or a clinical psychologist. I have worked in mental health for only a few years, teaching meditation and then qualifying as a hypnotherapist. I spent most of my career as a middle or senior manager in the packaged food industry, mostly in supply chain roles and some sales. It was partly my personal anxiety experiences which drove me to want to help myself, and in doing so, I realised that I could help others. I always enjoyed coaching my teams and seeing them succeed in what they do. It drove me more than hitting sales targets or making deliveries on time.

Burnout is an intangible concept in many ways. The word is sprinkled liberally into conversations about work, and Google searches on the term have doubled in the UK over the last five years (Ref. 4). The cause seems to be attributed mostly to work overload, and that is doubtless a key factor ... but we can't blame everything on external elements. We have human traits, too, which don't help us. In Chapter 2: Causes of Burnout, we will explore these dynamics, as well as throughout the book. Other mental illnesses such as depression are more likely to result from a chemical imbalance in the brain, historical trauma, or genetics, whereas burnout often comes from an external influence at work, or at least our reactions to it. Increasing pressures on businesses will only make this more challenging. As the screw slowly tightens, it is as if we are sleepwalking into a new pandemic. It is a virus that can be caught from the environment around us, and if our immune system is not up to scratch, we will let it invade us. It doesn't have to be permanent, however. One of the key reasons burnout happens is that it creeps up on us without us really being aware. It is exciting to begin an adventure of a new job or responsibility. But once we are on the ladder, it takes us in a specific direction, from which it is difficult to change course. There is a way back though. We just need to know the signs and have the mental armoury to extricate ourselves.

When a match burns out, it will not light again. It is different with us; there is healing and recovery, and there is most definitely hope. To avoid burnout or to recover from it, we must have resilience, and optimism is essential in a resilient person.

I love this quotation from Russian novelist, Fyodor Dostoevsky (Ref. 5).

*'You will burn, and you will burn out; you will be healed and come back again.'*

There is a distinct air of inevitability about this statement. The truth is that as humans we do need to challenge ourselves and be stimulated. It's not just the ever present need to keep earning money, that drives us to step over the line and take on too much. We learn from mistakes which are often made from pushing the envelope, from testing ourselves so that we grow. But it is comforting to think that there is a pathway back; a way to heal the wounds and live happily again. Burnout takes all the joy out of life. I hope that if you feel that this is the same for you (entirely plausible if you are reading a book on the topic), then you know that joy can and will return.

You can use the book in different ways. It is not only a guide to the stages of burnout and prevention, but also a workbook containing relevant tools; a living journal or document that you can keep with you always, as you go to the office or on the road. You could read all the way through from start to finish, as you would in a traditional book. Equally, you could flick through and look at the symptoms and characteristics of each stage of burnout and see what applies to you, then most importantly, see what the remedies are. I want you to peruse the buffet and take the morsels that are to your personal taste, because we are all different. There are 18 tools in the book. I wouldn't expect you to take them all on, or you might just be replacing one burnout problem with another.

The more I talk to people about burnout, the more prevalent it seems. It feels like something in the air that we can't actually sense, but is an ever-present danger.

I have read books about it, of course, in my research for this. I am an addicted reader of self-help books, principally since I am in the business myself. I hope this book is different in that it orientates the reader/sufferer, identifying their position on the map, then providing a compass and a destination.

*Alan Muskett*

*November 2024*

# CHAPTER 2
# CAUSES OF BURNOUT

## What is Burnout?

It makes sense to start with a definition. I suspect most of us think of being burned out as being physically exhausted with nothing left to give, like a spent pile of ashes. Burnout is often equated with depression since some of the symptoms are the same or at least similar. The lethargic lack of interest in anything in life, disconnecting socially, feeling tired all the time, are common to both conditions.

Although it is considered a modern phenomenon, using the phrase in the context of the mental state of a human being was coined in 1974 by Dr Herbert Freudenberger. In his book, *Burn-out: The High Cost of High Achievement*, published in 1980 (Ref. 6), he defined burnout as 'a state of fatigue or frustration that resulted from professional relationships that failed to produce the expected rewards'. In the days of Ancient

Greece, a condition existed which was very similar, known as *acedia*—defined as a 'state of listlessness,' but also as 'not seeming to care.' It was even defined as a sin by Pope Francis, not just because it seemed to equate with sloth, one of the Seven Deadly Sins, but also because a lack of caring about anything would spoil one's relationship with God.

Burnout, as defined by the World Health Organization (WHO, Ref. 7), has these key characteristics:

- Feelings of energy depletion or exhaustion
- Increased mental distance from one's job, or feelings of negativism or cynicism related to one's job
- Reduced professional efficacy

In the Deloitte UK report on mental health in 2022 mentioned in Chapter 1, two thirds of surveyed workers said they could identify with at least one of these characteristics, with 14% claiming that they were suffering with all three. The age bracket of 30–39 was most at risk, and especially women, who are more likely to be juggling responsibilities. Private sector workers were also shown to be much more likely to suffer.

The WHO definition would probably not be a surprise to anyone. If you are experiencing what you might deem to be burnout, you may be going through feelings of exhaustion or alienation from your work because you are sick and tired of it, the consequence of which means you are not as on the ball as you have been or could be. In researching this book, I have drawn much from a work by Australian psychiatrist Gordon Parker et al, and his book *A Guide to Identifying Burnout and Pathways to Recovery* (Ref. 8), based on what he called the Sydney Burnout Studies (Ref. 9), which took the existing definitions of burnout and uncovered some other factors. I have taken from his work and built on the WHO definition here.

Having interviewed thousands of self-diagnosed burnout sufferers, Parker's team realised that the WHO definition was simply too thin. The depth of what happens to us is inadequately conveyed by this list of three main symptoms. They seem to almost imply that the main sufferer of burnout might even be the employer. Of course, exhaustion is no fun if it is long-lasting and not the result of doing something highly satisfying. Having distance from a job might be seen as a bonus to millions of us, but of course, there are those who want to get satisfaction and meaning from their work. For many, our work actually defines us and who we are in life. The additional burnout factors from the Sydney Burnout Studies show that the full range of symptoms extend much deeper into us. If our 'work-self' is on the outside, then burnout punctures us on the inside, scarring deeply. Emotions are jarred, anxiety becomes an ever-present companion, and even our general cognitive powers start to wane, and that can be a terrifying prospect. We lack a sense of who we are, and why we do what we do. The table below summarises the WHO definitions above and the additional factors identified by Parker and his team. (Figure 1)

| WHO FACTORS | ADDITIONAL Sydney Burnout Studies Factors (and mine) |
|---|---|
| Exhaustion | Emotional exhaustion, anxiety |
| Distance from job, negativity, cynicism | Lack of care, lack of empathy, de-personalisation, dissociation, social withdrawal |
| Reduced professional efficacy | Cognitive impairment, general lethargy, and lack of interest in life |

*Figure 1. Factors associated with burnout.*

It is true that when you undertake research and keep asking questions, you will get more answers, and the symptoms may not necessarily relate to burnout but may be indicative of other pre-existing conditions. Nevertheless, the original definition looks light to me. It is much more serious than it looks at first glance, so we definitely should be taking a deeper dive.

Let's take the three main segments in turn.

1. **Exhaustion** can be a driver for many psychological problems. We only have to notice how we look at the world following a good night's sleep as opposed to a poor one. It is a physical problem that extends into a mental one and is often fleeting for a day or so. But if the exhaustion continues, then this is emotionally draining. By emotional exhaustion, I mean ex-

periencing so-called negative emotions such as sadness, grief, and guilt far too often and more intensely than we would like. As we will discover later, it is mentally healthy to allow this flavour of emotions to pass through us rather than blindly ignore them. However, there is a balance to be had, and we want to be experiencing more joy, pride, amusement, etc. The more we experience negative emotions, the more drained we will become in the long term.

Anxiety is a symptom, disorder, and phenomenon that is taking over the world. Again, we will explore further, but anxiety is a perfectly natural and useful emotion when we find ourselves standing by a busy street, holding tightly to a toddler's hand. Survival can depend upon a certain level of anxiety as a protection mechanism. But as with all emotions, it should pass by in relatively quick time. Chronic anxiety comes when stressing and worrying about life gets out of balance. It means we constantly worry about our future and become scared of it, predicting problems all the time. This is crippling and makes us avoid life, restricting our enjoyment of it. To be continually worried and scared of the future is to wear ourselves out.

2. The WHO refers to a **distance from the job and negativity** about it. Unfortunately, this lack of caring casts its shadow over all of the person we are. In the process of burning out, we

start to become cynical; not only about the job we are doing, but concerning anything in general. We are more sceptical about politicians (if that is possible), about ourselves, and about the intentions of others. This is because a constant flow of negative emotions through us influences the way we think. As tiredness and irritability become rampant, we are less likely to believe that anyone else is capable of doing good things, much less ourselves. This is where we stop caring, lose empathy, and therefore, withdraw socially, which is a vital stage of burnout. We start to lose a sense of ourselves and who we are, as our view on the world becomes ever more insular and disconnected.

3. Finally, there is **professional efficacy.** The WHO refers to not being able to do the job properly, but this applies equally to remembering to buy all the groceries needed for the weekend or forgetting people's names in social situations. In burnout, the brain has been hijacked for emotional crisis, and our memory and cognitive ability is far from being effective. This means we are cognitively impaired and lose concentration, become forgetful, and become less adept at problem solving.

I would sum up these three segments like this then, adding in those other factors.

## Physical Exhaustion and Negative Emotions
## Cynicism and Losing a Sense of Self
## Cognitive Impairment and Lacking Enjoyment in Life

Nobody wants to be described in these terms, but these are the common traits that we can expect to feel when we are burning out. There is more at stake than just what happens with our jobs. I hate the thought of someone being tossed on the scrap heap after all the productivity has been squeezed out of them, but this is what companies do unfortunately, and in a world ever more obsessed with greed over balance, it will become ever more so.

It is, however, understandable that the job aspect is focused upon. Work yields money which provides food, shelter, entertainment, status, and gravitas. We spend most of our time working or thinking about it when we are in full time employment. We are all different in this respect and have diverging needs. For some, our jobs define us, and we rely on our success professionally to feel fulfilled. There is nothing wrong with that. The burnout factors bleed into all our lives. If we are burned out at work, then we feel negative and cynical about all of our relationships, personal and social ones too. We are not effective at *anything*. Interest in life really is at rock bottom.

Work may be the cause of burnout, or it may just be a part of the problem, which lies somewhere else. The health care profession is riddled with burnout, and there has been plenty of media coverage pointing out the plight of our underpaid doctors and nurses. But there are those who slip between the cracks. In the so-called sandwich generation, many are holding down demanding full-time jobs, bringing up families in an increasingly complicated and terrifying world, and becoming amateur carers for a sick parent, for example. My mum looked after my dad when he had Parkinson's. In the beginning, she had a full-time job too, but then she retired as it all got too much. I stepped in for her once a year while she had a weekend break, and it was tough. He was wheelchair-bound and needed to be hoisted in and out of bed, and into the shower. It would sometimes take me an hour just to get him dressed. It was exhausting, even if it was rewarding. But that was for a long weekend. Imagine doing it day in, day out, while balancing all your other responsibilities. This is also a route to burnout that the WHO definition doesn't really factor in.

Let's not worry too much about the distinction, therefore, between work and other causes. Humans are complicated anyway. It is not easy to discern exactly what bothers us, and it can change day by day, moment by moment. We are a mash-up of thoughts, emotions, feelings, and beliefs. Nowadays, boundaries between work and home are blurred, and we bleed problems from one environment into another as we battle with them. We should simply be aware of these as human experiences and have the space and freedom to take the right action for us when it is required. This book is about discovering what you need and being able to do something about it.

## Who is most at risk?

I almost did not put this small section in, because it doesn't matter what job you are in, you can burnout if the circumstances are getting on top of you. So please don't be offended if you are having a tough time and not in one of these professions. Nevertheless, this chapter would not be complete if I didn't include them! So here they are, according to the Sydney studies.

Professions with significant inherent burnout risk are:

- Health care (no surprises, we all remember COVID-19)
- Teachers (nor for this, I am surprised we have any left)
- Lawyers (who seem to work VERY long hours)
- Police (no surprise, working with their life on the line every day)
- Senior Managers (constant demands from boards and shareholders)

*(Source: Sydney Burnout Studies, Gordon Parker)*

But if you are not in this list, it doesn't mean you can't burnout, of course. Carers are not listed but as stated above, it is not always a full-time profession. It is something done in between answering emails, attending Teams calls, and running a household. If you do work in one of these professions above, then you should be extra vigilant at seeking help if you feel you are having difficulties. If you're not in one, read on anyway. It's only a guide, and misleading to think that burnout is isolated to specific job types.

## Why does burnout happen?

There is a simple answer to this and also a very long one. For the long answer, I say that this is to be discovered in the rest of this book. The simple answer is that burnout is a human response to excessive and chronic stress (the type that hangs around for a long time and doesn't let up). We burn out because, as the WHO puts it (Ref. 7), 'Burn-out is a syndrome conceptualized as resulting from chronic workplace stress that has not been successfully managed.' This means that a burnout sufferer is overwhelmed by demands placed upon them and does not have the resources to be able to cope with the stress effectively. It is a simple enough statement, but there are many reasons why we allow the resulting stress to get to us, which is essentially what this book is about. We can't necessarily take away the factors which cause the stresses, but we can be aware of and change our reaction to them.

## Reacting to danger: the stress response

As we've responded to threats in our environment we have evolved, over hundreds of millions of years, a stress response. This is to get the body into gear to fight for one's life, or to run like hell for it. It is a magnificent tool for survival and is deployed rapidly if we are in danger.

In the limbic part of our brains (a characteristic we share with other mammals), we have, in both hemispheres, a small, almond-shaped cluster of neurons called the *amygdala*. This has a number of functions, but primarily is involved in detecting threat to us as an organism. We share this function with other animal species, of course, and the mechanism has been designed by nature to avoid danger and move towards safety–either by fighting or running away. You may have heard of this as the *fight-or-flight* response.

If the amygdala detects a threat, it will sound an internal alarm, and a chain reaction of events will result in the adrenal glands secreting a stress-chemical, *cortisol*. This hormone is a glucocorticoid and raises blood sugar levels, increases the supply of blood to major muscles so we can run or fight, and turns off systems not needed in that situation, such as digestion and immune function. All of this happens very fast too - in a fraction of a second from detecting a threat, we are ready for action, whatever that might be. This is a perfectly honed defence mechanism when fleeing from a predator or grappling with a burglar, but the thing about the amygdala is, it cannot tell the difference between a real threat–a threat to our life–or a perceived one such as getting a nastygram from the Sales Director. This is not a threat to our existence. Yet, either way, it will kick into life, much like a smoke alarm. It will react in exactly the same way when our house is on fire, or if we have just burned the toast. If it keeps going off, when we have had an argument, spilled some coffee on our computer, feel as if we are being left out of a friend group, then soon the batteries will wear out on the alarm. And so it is with our bodies. A system designed by nature for extreme action (required only once in a while) has been overwound in modern life. Our delicate systems have been hacked!

Stress is good; we need it to get us into action. But not all the time, and if our body's healing processes are compromised when we are in chronic stress, then we are going to see some harm develop. An immune system consistently compromised means more illnesses; some minor, some very serious. It has been suggested that 'burnout' might be an appropriate term for the syndrome, since sufferers, after prolonged periods of cortisol production, may stop producing it. This is known as *hypocortisolism*, and it would explain why we become tired and fatigued in later stages of burning out, since we are not producing the get-up-and-go fuel that we need. The adrenals have essentially burned out. As cortisol plays a role in reducing inflammation, then it might also explain why we suffer more aches and pains, which may not have any obvious biological cause. It's a hypothesis though, as the connection has not yet been made in tests, but absence of evidence doesn't mean evidence of absence! The theory fits the symptoms at least, as we shall see when we follow the path to burnout.

## Whose fault is burnout anyway?

It's a complicated topic allocating blame for burnout. Is it us or them? The world is competitive and demanding by its laws of life. We are only here because we have, as a species, been able to adapt to our environment and do it better than other life forms. If we weren't demanding of ourselves and others, we may not be in that exalted position. We might feel that we are being burned out in a toxic culture, and simultaneously berating ourselves for allowing it to happen. Individual behaviour and group behaviour are interlinked, and there is no beginning or end to that circle. If we are competitive as individuals, it is because we need to be keeping up with the tribe. The group will keep the individual accountable, and so we develop behaviours and systems that make us successful in surviving within that tribe. We are a part of a connected system. Humans tend to follow certain modes of behaviour to ensure they survive. It's a rollercoaster that's difficult to get off if we wanted to.

What I am saying here is that it is pointless blaming a toxic culture or manager for our burnout. We cannot control the environment we are dropped into, not in the near term anyway, but we can control our response to it. It is within this sense of *response*-ability that determines whether we will succumb to burnout or not. I don't want to turn off anyone who is suffering from burnout by just dismissing their problems as of their own making. Not at all. I am saying the problems are caused by a system of operation in which we work, and the solution always lies within oneself. We have the power to change ourselves, and consequently, the environment around us.

It might be the first thing that leaps to mind when

someone says they're burned out. They have been placed under too much pressure by their greedy (or desperate) employer, and don't have the capacity to cope. That is certainly true in many cases since there is simply too much to do sometimes given the time, resources, and tools that we have at our disposal. If you give me eight hours' worth of gardening to do, but only four hours to do it in, then my ability to do the job is compromised. Depending on my personality, I might approach the job in different ways. I could just plod on until my allotted four hours is up. I could spend a few minutes planning, and prioritise the tasks that simply must be done and leave the nice to do's until next time. Or, I could rush around the garden at double speed, trying to get it all done, even if I make a few mistakes along the way. I may even deploy a mix of these different tactics as I work through the time allowed.

We are all different, and we will approach it in correspondingly different ways. Some of us may agonise over our compromised results, or the cloud hanging over us of work not completed. Others may simply walk away and move on, not giving it a second thought. I wonder which of all these personality types would be more prone to burnout. What do you think? In Chapter 6: Rung 1: Ignition, I explain perfectionism and its significant role here. Spending life rushing around and trying to be all things to all people, trying to do things exceedingly well so no one can criticise—wouldn't you worry for that person? Is that person you?

## Some of our major flaws—human mind traps

I am not blaming you *per se*, but to be honest, there are a few flaws which your highly sophisticated brain has designed and built over the endless millennia of your evolution. They could be at least partly responsible for any burnout risk, so I will highlight them here.

## Survival and the negative bias

What are we here for? Really? Some might say to be happy, others that we are simply here to survive long enough to pass our genes on to the next generation and contribute to the prolonging of our species. Our brains have given us the fundamental tools we need to cannily navigate this tricky world. Human beings are not particularly fast or strong compared to other members of the animal kingdom, but our ability to think, and think about thinking, has given us the decisive edge in our quest to survive. And that is what we are programmed to do. Stubbornly and bloody-mindedly. But to do that, fairly tragically, we have needed to adopt a negative, survival-focused mindset.

Are we meant to be happy (by 'happy,' I mean a sense of overall well-being combined with satisfaction and joy)? Well, as we progress through a hierarchy of needs (see pages 87–88 in Chapter 6: Rung 1: Ignition), first ensuring our basic safety and survival, all the way to self-actualisation and fulfilment, then perhaps yes. But first, we need to ensure the basics are in place. Maslow's Hierarchy of Needs (Ref. 10) is often depicted visually as a pyramid, with safety providing the foundation at the base. We can't take away that layer and expect the pyramid to stay standing. If we don't continue to maintain our own safety, then we can forget about happiness. A *homo sapiens* adult may feel a sense of contentment sitting round the fire after filling his belly with food, but he may have one eye in the bushes for a nasty attacker from a rival tribe or a beast with large teeth. While looking out upon a beautiful landscape in the evening twilight, he may fix his eyes on a beige-looking rock in the distance and worry that it may be a stalking lion. The beauty is forgotten, the danger in sharp focus. So it is with us in modern-day life. As stated before, this does not apply to real danger necessarily, but we humans will focus on negative points in case they trip us up. It may be a mainly blue sky while relaxing on the beach, but a dark cloud coming overhead will have us thinking about where we might get shelter from the rain. If we do a presentation at work, and we are praised for the result, we will still focus on the part where they said we weren't very clear. That is what we will dwell on as we drive home.

We have developed a habitual partiality for looking for these faults in ourselves, just as a virus checker on a computer routinely looks for problems. For us, this constant scanning for danger is a natural survival technique. If the beige-looking rock *was* a lion, then that ancestor had a better chance of passing on their genes than someone who just relaxed and thought everything was safe. This hardwired code keeps us moving and keeps us improving, but it also drains us of energy. We need it, clearly, or we will become complacent and irrelevant. But if we let it dominate, it will get on top of us, keeping us in fight-or-flight unnecessarily. It exhausts us by keeping those alarm systems running and warps our view of the world. We will consistently err on the side of seeing lions rather than rocks.

## People Pleasing and Boundary Setting

A classic comment I hear in the therapy or training room is, 'I am a people-pleaser.' It is such an odd term, particularly juxtaposed against our natural in-built need to ensure our own survival first. That is the desire of the individual's brain, of course. We have all seen news footage where we are shown people who have lost their homes after a devastating tsunami or other natural disaster. We think to ourselves, 'Poor people. I am so lucky; I must learn to enjoy life more and be more grateful for what I have.' In that moment, we are full of empathy. Then a power cut disconnects the Wi-Fi and we can't access the internet, and then we are cursing the utility providers and wondering how we are going to 'survive' the day. All thoughts of some poor parent clutching a bewildered toddler while looking at the rubble of their house are dismissed. The immediate problem is right in front of us and that is what we focus on—the comparatively minor disturbance to our day. This shows how egotistical and shallow we are. We only care about ourselves. Yet, we are also people-pleasers. The twist in this is that we are that way in order to enable our own survival. We manipulate others to get what we want. To be part of a tribe is to be accepted, and this means there are certain responsibilities which we undertake to make sure we are looked upon as useful. Activities such as lighting a fire, cooking a meal, bringing home food, keeping the house clean, are all fairly primitive pastimes which we do today as we did all those millennia ago. The pride we feel is a reward for the brain and body–a reminder to do it again. It makes us feel good about being useful, and we will perhaps even do more of it. We begin to fall over ourselves, crossing boundaries to help someone for whom we need some kind of validation, whether it is a partner or a boss, sacrificing our own self-care and wearing ourselves out. We do it so that we may survive. Because it is so hard-wired into our tribal mentality, so many of us are people-pleasers and fail to set appropriate boundaries. We would rather give away too much than too little so that we don't risk antagonising someone or not getting the validation reward. If we don't address this, it will erode at our resilience and energy, and eventually, self-respect.

## Model making and our predictive brains

In an uncertain world where we might need to defend ourselves against predators at a moment's notice, we have a requirement for ensuring that whatever is around us in our environment is safe. We need to be able to *predict* that matters will stay that way. If we had a weather forecast to help us decide if we need to take an umbrella out with us today, then any such prediction is based upon a mathematical model. These are built from masses of historical data, from which patterns are analysed, and then, as if in a meat grinder, calculated into a projection forward. Our brains work in the same way. We use the past to predict the future, and we do this by building mental models of the world in which we live. We do this to enable our survival so that we might be able to anticipate danger ahead of us.

## What is a mental model?

The map we create in our heads is necessary, simply because we need to make sense of an incredibly complex world. But what we have in our heads, for example is only ever an approximation of reality. For example, we may have a model we create mentally of what our workplace looks like, and we might think that is pretty accurate. We have, after all, entered that physical space many times before. The thing is, we can't possibly take in all of the information available, as it would be too much for the brain to handle at any one time—the colour of the carpets, the walls, the sounds in the building, the hum of the people, the feel of the air, the touch of the door handle as we open it to go into the office. Much of this is fairly irrelevant information, since we are more concerned about the meeting we are just about to have, so all of our cognitive power is diverted to that. The building we go in does not generally provide any risk to our survival, so we don't need to consciously think about it. Why bother taking in all that infinite detail? We therefore have a mental model of the workplace built up of approximations.

## Nothing is real

Not only do we approximate the outside environment depending on what we are truly interested in, we live in a simulated world inside our heads. Think about it, no part of the brain is directly connected with the outside environment. It relies on extremely sophisticated simulations to build up a picture of what is around us. There is no such thing as colour in the universe as we know it. Our eyes interpret different frequencies of light hitting our cones (photoreceptor cells on the retina), which send electrical signals to the brain, interpreting the light as colours. There is no sound either; only vibrations in the air picked up by the ear drum, again signalled electronically to the brain and interpreted as noises which we can magically discern. Sensory receptors help us identify smells, touch, taste, all of which are interpreted by the brain to create an assessment of what is happening in any given moment that we 'understand'. So, our models of the world are never going to be 100% accurate, yet we use them to predict what's coming.

Where this really starts to become relevant to the matter at hand, namely burnout and stress unmanaged, is that we create mental models not just of the sensory details around us—the sights, the sounds, the smells and so on. We create maps of *situations*, those that we might be facing in the future, but based on our experience of the past and our interpretations of the world. If our data is inaccurate then we can't forecast the 'weather', and may end up getting caught in the rain, or worse perhaps, not enjoying the sun because we are dressed for a storm.

## Making memories

Where do we get our data from for our own models and forecasts? From the past of course, from all of our experiences, which in turn come from our memories. Science is still discovering how we create our memories, but what is already known is that they are not just pulled from a file like a photograph, a factual record of an event. They are recreated from different parts of the brain and influenced by our associations and even current moods. My recollection of an event is most often different from yours, and no wonder if this is our method of recall. It's fantastically intricate and complex, but it means that our memories often let us down too in creation of our models. So just a side note here which will come up time and again in later chapters. We must remember that our models are created from simulations and experiences which cannot be 100% accurate, and therefore we build faulty models from which to base our predictions.

Bad memories will skew a model and dispropor-tionately affect our predictions. If you invite me to an annual dinner-dance that I have never been to, my mind will prepare me by building up a picture of what that is going to be like, and how I will keep myself safe. I may have a picture from a film or a book of what it might be like, and I will start to anticipate how it will be according to this model I am creating. I will need to dress appropriately, brush up on my table manners, and keep up with the news so that I may make small talk. I may even have to dust off my dancing skills. All this planning comes from a model which will be inaccurate but possibly good enough to see me through.

The issue with model-making is that it means we go into situations with a pre-disposed view of how events will play out. If we are nervous of going to dinner-dances, it may be because we have memories of previously embarrassing experiences. We trod on someone's toes as we quick-stepped, and now this forms part of our mental model as something to be aware of. It will make us tighten up with nerves, perhaps avoid dancing at all on the night, and all because there was just one occasion where we didn't get it quite right. The bad memory has distorted the model, bent it out of shape. But unfortunately, that becomes our map, our navigation aid for the dinner dance.

This happens in life all the time. We have models in our heads of situations we don't like and people we can't stand, and because of our negative bias, we tend to focus on the negative aspects because they are the parts that threaten us. They become outsized features in the model, way bigger than they should be, inaccurate and not based on reality.

## We are all control freaks

We have a need to be on top of what is going on around us for obvious reasons. To have our mental map represent something which looks like safety to us. There is the way the world is and the way we want it to be, and if there is a gap between the two, we look to close it. It results in us trying to manipulate the world to be in line with our view, with our model. This could be as simple as being cold, and wanting to be warm, putting on a sweater to manipulate our body temperature. It could also be when we desperately want a politician to win (or lose) an election, because we might be threatened by the potential actions of this unwanted leader. The world we live in is vast and situations are mostly out of our control, yet our need to be safe dictates that we try to manipulate it as much as we can, leading to us interfering in situations which would otherwise just unfold. We worry about the effects of an outcome because it contravenes our view of the world, which although we have seen is flawed, is to be vehemently protected. We have a need to be right, that our model is correct, and so this leads us to entrench our beliefs and refuse to be open to different possibilities.

## Filling in the gaps

Not only do we need to believe our model is right, but it must also be complete. If you find you can't walk past an unfinished jigsaw puzzle without attempting to fit a few pieces, then this is what the brain itself is like. An incomplete picture represents potential danger. Back to the lion/rock example. If our eyesight is not good enough to see that far, our mental model may already contain a possibility that a lion exists outside of our range of vision. Because we can't update the model with reality and conclude either way, we will most likely keep the possibility of a stalking lion in the distance in the model-thereby meaning we can't relax even when we could.

Therefore, human beings do not like information gaps. When we don't have all the information relating to our environment or what we are focusing on at the time, then we tend to fill those gaps in with our imaginations or find ways to manipulate our environment for control purposes. For example, it is thought that human language was developed so that we could gossip about other members of our tribe. In groups of about 150 people, it is possible to recognise everybody but not know everyone in any great depth. So, if we wanted to find out about that shifty-looking character who hangs around the circle by the campfire but never actually acknowledges us, then we might start to ask questions to others. Are they friendly? Can they be trusted? What do they bring to us? In this scenario, we are attempting to control or at least update our model of the tribe, by staying up to date with the latest on our peers. And, if we didn't get the information we were looking for, then we would invoke our imagination and deploy that species-defining skill: storytelling. We dream up the story of what is going on by filling in the gaps of what we don't know, and we create something which might require action from us. In the tribe, if a person hasn't been seen for days, then we might think they are up to something—plotting, making weapons, or stealing food. We could exert control by spying on them and reporting them to others if we thought they were dangerous. It might just turn out that they had been ill and needed to be alone and quiet somewhere away from camp. In that case, reality turned out differently than the story we made up. But because of the propensity to think the worst-case scenario due to our negative bias, then the tales we create don't often help that much in reality. But if the tribe member really was off doing something Machiavellian, then we would be ready, wouldn't we? We would have predicted the danger and most likely been ready for it. But how much of our precious energy did it take to do that when it was not ultimately necessary. And think of the precious moments we missed while we were not present with life.

## Everyone loves a good story

Stories help us put things into order in our heads. We use metaphors to illustrate concepts, and this is how the brain can organise the facts in our heads. Aesop's Fables were a powerful way to demonstrate ethics and morals by appealing to this way of learning. We become emotionally involved in the story too. Actors in dramas on TV will talk lines written for them by someone else, yet emotionally, we believe that what is behind the screen is true. We feel outraged when a villain gets away with a crime, even though we know we are being fed an illusion. And as we have just discussed, if any aspect of a story is missing, then we need to fill it in.

Consider this simple scenario:

You are in the pub, and you see three people you know who are close friends. You also know that they are going to a party that night because you also know the host—you are not going because you are working later. You say hello and let them get on with their chat. Here are some factual statements about the situation, including that which transpired afterward. Read them through and notice what you make of it.

- The three friends were due to go to a party
- They were seen happily talking in the pub
- One took a phone call and looked quite upset
- Only two of the friends later turned up to the party

What thoughts come to mind for you? Notice how you need to know what's going on? All seemed well, then someone takes a phone call, and something bad has clearly happened. Has someone had an accident? Gone to hospital, maybe? Have they died? Maybe the upset one just got dumped. Notice how your mind reaches for logical explanations. Look how quickly you conjure up scenarios for the information you are not aware of. Be aware, too, how you have assumed from the facts that it was the one who took the phone call that didn't go to the party ... come on, I know you thought that.

It is this need to know which is both a blessing and a curse for a human being. Our thirst for knowledge and curiosity has given us the ability to discover wondrous things about the universe around us. But can't it make us anxious too? How much time do you spend anticipating what others are thinking and plotting? When we haven't heard from someone for a long time, it is easy to jump to the conclusion that they don't like us anymore—because we said something to upset them, or maybe because we haven't said anything at all. Then, when we talk to them and find out they are happy and friendly, and have just been incredibly busy, the information gap is filled in and it is no longer a problem to us. It is our endless ruminations in which we invent stories that causes us such anguish. It is the need to know and the need to be safe in our environment which leads to this. If someone doesn't like me, I am not safe. It could mean, in the world of a hunter-gatherer, that I might be murdered in my sleep or expelled from the group. The chances of this happening to us are fortunately much more obscure in modern life, but our brains haven't moved on so much, despite their incredible complexity.

## What's this got to do with burnout?

I hope you found those last paragraphs on human mind traps interesting, but I don't want you to think I have strayed too far from the topic at hand–burnout. In my view, these behavioural traits have a hand in making our lives more difficult and get us into more trouble as we try to make sense of the world, which often is all we are trying to do. They are not the only causes of burnout, and others are explored later in the book, but I believe these mind traps, that arise from distorted views of reality, contribute to our downfall. They deprive us of energy and cause us to behave in strange ways.

## Mind trap summary

**Negative Bias**–because of our primary need for survival, we have a tilt towards negativity and self-criticism as a way of telling us to pull our own socks up. It leads us to prepare for dangers that don't really exist (the smoke alarm), thus wasting our energy.

**Hunter-Gatherer (Tribal) Mindset**–we exist and operate in tribes in the same way our ancient ancestors did—then, as now, it was necessary to be cooperative and useful. We carry this to an extreme and can overextend our personal boundaries. It also means that we might behave in a way which impresses others ahead of ourselves, so we lose our sense of authenticity and ability to follow our own values.

**Predictive brains and model making**–as we know, our brains need to make predictions of the future based on the past, which is based on simulations of reality and inaccuracies. These models form our beliefs and shape the way we behave in situations and with people. We can get stuck in habitual thought patterns which jar with reality and prevent us seeing things as they actually are. This means we go into situations with incorrect assumptions and make mistakes because of them. It stops us enjoying life sometimes, just because our models are influenced by negative bias.

**The need for control**–like it or not, we are ALL control freaks so that we may feel safe in our environment. We want things to be a certain way and so will manipulate where possible, so we can achieve that. We need this because we want the world to conform with our values and beliefs. A common problem among clients I see is that they worry when they are not in control. But we can't be in control of everything, and it not only drains us to try, but we also lose focus in what we do if we can't let go of the uncontrollable.

**Storytelling**–if we don't have control and information is missing, we can assume the worst. Our wondrous ability to imagine leads us to tell stories to ourselves and create fictions about the scenarios we live in which are just not very helpful. We believe in stories because that is often how we learn and establish our models in the first place.

Human beings act the way we do because we have needs as individuals which drives us to perform in a certain manner in groups. The group dynamic then in turn influences the way individuals behave. So, it's a circle that has no real beginning or end. We can't really blame the system or even ourselves because we are dependent on each other. Being aware of our human shortcomings is helpful though, and as you will see, awareness is a key theme in this book. Especially as burnout is a phenomenon that can lure us in and eat us up as we sleepwalk into it.

# CHAPTER 3
# THE TOXIC WORKPLACE

**If you are a manager/leader/employer, then read on. This is a segment on how to avoid a toxic workplace, allow employees to thrive, and avoid burnout.**

**If you are an employee, read on too, since this is what you need to expect in a workplace as a basic minimum.**

As discussed in the last chapter, there is no simple answer to 'is it us or them?' That said, workplaces cause burnout if the environment is not right, because their atmospheres can trigger those human frailties and mind traps. There are great places to work and there are terrible ones, and opinions on that differ based on each individual's experiences. Sometimes it's not the overall culture that is at fault, but one manager. Research has tended to show that people leave managers rather than companies, but that doesn't mean the onus is entirely on the individual boss to provide a nurturing environment. Workplaces are an ecosystem, and managers and individuals can only thrive in the right conditions provided. This is usually driven by leadership teams, and it is incumbent upon them to support their managers to do right by their people.

## Managers are struggling to cope with stress and worry

A recent report by AXA in the UK has shown that 33% of line managers have taken time off due to mental health problems (Ref. 11). I am both encouraged and discouraged by this. Staggered that the toll is so high, but refreshed that people do take time off when they need it. In a previous company I worked for, employees were allowed to take PC (Personal Choice) days; two days in a year where they did not have to justify an absence but could just not turn in if they did not feel like it. Perhaps we could relabel this as a 'mental resilience day' and make it a national obligation for employers. A report by Gallup in 2024 (Ref. 12) showed that managers have more 'negative experiences' than non-managers— these are defined as stress, worry, sadness, loneliness, and anger. There is a heavy bias towards the first two words in that list, which are symptoms that, if left unchecked, will certainly contribute to burnout. The other three words are alarming too, however, and could be a sign that burnout is well advanced.

A report by The Wellbeing Project, *The Manager Resilience Report*, in 2024 (Ref. 13), showed that pinch points for line managers are high working volumes and hours, too much organisational change, and a feeling of being undervalued. Line managers' resilience is compromised by a lack of energy—a burnout symptom driven by work volume and hours. They are also struggling with getting their basics right, such as poor nutrition, exercise, and sleep. Senior managers and leaders complain of a lack of work/life balance, driven by a high volume of work too. And according to Gallup, leaders are suffering the most from burnout, with one in four saying they feel burned out 'often or always,' and two in three feeling it 'sometimes.'

Engaged managers/leaders equals engaged employees. If we can't help everyone with mental health or resilience training, then companies can get a huge bang for their buck by reaching the squeezed line managers. The payback will be monumental, or at least around 5:1, as Deloitte have shown.

## Setting the right workplace conditions

Dr. Christina Maslach, a psychology professor from University of California, Berkeley, is highly respected in the field of burnout study and even has a measure named after her, the Maslach Burnout Inventory. I am not going into that in this book, simply because it opens up cans of worms that you shouldn't have to deal with. To go into the pros and cons of it would not be valuable here. In any case, this book is not a statistical study, but a practical help guide to avoid burnout. My purpose is not to get us bogged down. As you will see, I have developed my own burnout assessment measure, which you can take yourself. This will give you the starting point and the guidance you need to follow in the book and the coaching programme should you choose to work with me. I have found this suits clients well. I do recommend spending just over half an hour listening to Dr. Maslach's talk on YouTube via this QR code (Ref. 14).

But if you don't have 37 minutes to spare, I will summarise it for you here very succinctly, I hope!

## The magnificent 7 of employee satisfaction (and by default—burnout avoidance)

Dr. Maslach discusses the following seven factors which might lead to those defined WHO burnout outcomes outlined earlier. There is a similarity with a widely accepted practice that an employee has certain needs to be able to do their job properly (not to mention, live their life in a state of normalcy and contentment, rather than anxiety and frustration). Credit where credit is due; one of my employers used to ensure that many of these questions were asked of the employee at an annual performance review. They were intended as an opportunity to voice, by way of feedback, to their manager that their needs were being met and enabling them to do their job. Back then (this was 20 years ago), few people were talking about their mental health needs or risks of burnout. Nevertheless, it was some decent thinking on how to check if employees were getting the space that they needed to do their job.

Those questions focused on if they were getting support from their manager, if they had the room to manoeuvre, if they had some control and agency, and finally, if they were getting recognition for what they did. Dr. Maslach's seven factors below extend these by covering the environment more than the individual's personalised needs, but they don't really cover the support from the manager. If workload can be managed, that may be a contribution from the manager, but I am referring to the softer skills: the art of listening without judgement and providing psychological safety for the employee (that is, to be able to communicate openly and take risks without fear of reprisal). The manager has a tricky balance of ensuring accountability and showing empathy for the individual. Some really struggle with one or the other. Some can be tough, and others give love. Tough love, on the other hand, is not always easy!

Below, I have laid out Dr. Maslach's seven factors, but the words accompanying them are my own viewpoints and experiences.

## Workplace-caused burnout

1. **Overextended Workload:** This is the most obvious cause of burnout and one that most of

us would picture if we thought about it—the individual, burning the candle at both ends, buried under workload and meetings, brain fried with the sheer relentlessness of it all. This is what worries us most when we go into a new job or project. Do I have the capacity to get it all done? Do I have the capability to get through this without it burying me? There is the problem of the opposite to this, of course, and that is **Underextended Workload.** It can cause a great deal of stress when we don't have enough to do, as it can erode our confidence and self-worth. We can be spinning our wheels by getting stressed about it, even though there is no need to burn mental fuel. Nowadays of course, there are very few places where someone can be so consistently under-utilised, but it does happen when work systems and flows aren't clicking. If you are waiting for somebody else to do something on a task before passing it on to you, and all the time the deadline is looming larger, this is stressful. Vital energy gets wasted as we have time to think about the possibilities of a poor outcome, rather than simply being able to get on with it.

Bizarrely, some of us don't have enough to do. I have heard a term recently to describe this, known as 'bore-out.' Sometimes, there's nothing worse than having too much time to think. This one is for managers, in the first instance. However well an organisation designs its structures to do the work, pockets will appear of overextended and underextended workload. The manager's skill is to rebalance or make decisions over what has to give. They need, therefore, the empowerment to be able to push back on other departments or more senior managers to say whether they are over-capacity already. They also need to have the capability and autonomy to redesign workflows to rebalance. Which leads me to workplace environment Cause 2.

2. Lack of **Agency:** Agency means the ability to influence an outcome; a degree of *control* over what we are doing, and the chance to make decisions and have the space to perform. There is little worse than feeling as if you have no say in what actions you can take, even in the most mundane of tasks. Most of us take pride in what we do, and as we do more of it, we like to get better at it, making changes here and there to make us more effective or efficient. If we operate within parameters so tight that we have little or no power, this erodes our enjoyment and self-worth, and we tie ourselves up in an echo chamber of complaining. Managers need to trust that an employee knows their job best and give them some freedom. Of course, with that comes a different level of accountability, and each needs to know expectations of the other. But with some risk comes reward, and this is a hugely important factor.

3. Lack of **Role Clarity:** We all like to think that we can write clear job descriptions and that roles can be so clearly defined, but as companies get larger and more complex, this becomes incredibly difficult. Frustrations occur when people step over each other, duplicating tasks, and also when gaps appear because no one is taking responsibility. Both can be due to politics and ego, as well as organisational dysfunction. Leaders can be heard telling their teams, 'That's *our* job, not theirs,' or conversely, 'No way are we touching that!' as they battle for position on what can make them most successful over and above their peers. Sometimes it can just be a lack of effective communication or understanding. Whatever the cause, the individual needs to be able to put up their hand and say, 'I don't know what my job is!' (thereby demonstrating Agency too).

4. Lack of **Reward** (recognition more importantly than remuneration): This taps into a basic human need of validation that we are doing a good job. Money rewards are short-lived in terms of motivation, since we quickly adapt to slightly increased salaries, or we blow a bonus on a holiday or a car. I only remember one significant monetary reward I got, particularly because it was a whopper, but what I treasure even more was the phone call from my CEO to tell me personally that I had done a remarkable job on a high-profile project. It is that which stays with

me. We are like puppies sometimes. We love a pat on the head and the occasional treat, but for us, the delivery needs to be sincere, and I am usually suspicious of forced gratitude and weekly shout-outs to 'employees of the week.' Spontaneity is key, and insincerity is more damaging than not saying anything at all. Public 'thank you's' can be demotivating for those that feel that they should have got one and didn't. If you're a leader, think carefully about how such incentives are utilised, and aim for consistency.

5. Community **Dysfunction:** Most of us hate it when we don't get on with others, either within a team or when tribal warfare breaks out. We spend most of our lives with people we work with, and as humans, we are wired to connect and cooperate. There are, of course, those that create toxicity by fostering discord for their own protection or gain. Most of us just want to have a pleasant environment and get on with our jobs, then go home to our personal lives. If that is threatened, then so are we, leaving us feeling stressed by it, and burnout can follow. It is more difficult in these hybrid work-from-home times, and it is less likely that teams will be able to get together and build bonds socially, so managers need to be creative on this.

6. Lack of **Fairness:** The world is unfair, but it doesn't mean that we are not outraged when un-

fairness is evident. Here, we are talking about disparities in the way team members are treated, or between departments. We have a natural tendency as individuals to try and evenly administer kindness, resources, rewards, attention. As kids, we grow up with a sense of what is fair and what is not. It makes us cry and it makes us mad. We feel threatened if we perceive that others get better perks than we do, even if we feel our contribution to the effort is just as key. I always had a beef with the treatment that sales teams get for hitting a target, when other departments trail in their wake when it comes to hospitality benefits, or as we used to call them, 'jollies.' (I seemed to discard this sanctimony when I was in sales, however. I am only human, after all.) I suppose CFO's and anti-competition laws (leading to fewer customer perks) have lowered the common denominator so that nobody gets much of this these days, and it is less of an issue. When it seems that the deck is stacked against us or our teams for whatever reason, the best way to protect our mental state is to not worry about what we cannot control (see Chapter 10: Rung 5: Disengage), but it still bothers people, and leaders need to be aware of the impacts of preferential treatment.

7. Incongruent with **Values:** We will get a boost if we can connect with the values of our organisation and if it matches ours, ethically speak-

ing. Is what we are doing making a difference for good in the world? It depends on our own motivations of course; how important is this for us? I remember a boss of mine telling our team that he had noticed a vacancy had come up selling cigarettes for a tobacco company. I didn't fancy it, to be honest, but he said he had no issue with it. We are all different, but in this age of information and transparency, people are becoming more aware and therefore, we have greater control over where we work and for what reasons. If we have a strong sense of ethics or values and there is a mismatch with the organisation, it will create anxiety and could be a burnout factor.

## A good boss can counterbalance a toxic workplace

As I said in an earlier paragraph, there is a missing piece in this list which comes in the form of an empathetic leader. You could argue that if all the other needs are met as described above, this indicates that a manager is doing their job. I think, however, that it needs to be spelled out, as there are so many inadequately trained and uncaring managers about, that it would be remiss not to state what might seem to be the obvious. There is an obligation for a manager to balance ensuring the employee is delivering against their goals, but also to facilitate an atmosphere of safety and a nurtured environment where the employee can flourish. They also need to recognise that employees need feedback on their performance regularly, and not just be surprised at their annual performance review. It is staggering how often this happens. As I said earlier, people leave bosses, they don't leave companies. Although we might focus on a toxic culture, which is a collective disease in a company, there might still be some rotten apples in an otherwise healthy basket.

With so many managers struggling (remember: one in three going off with mental health issues!), there is a clear case for better training, both in management itself, and for personal resilience to stress.

## Boss—lend me your ear (not a solution)

In Gordon Parker's work in the Sydney Burnout Studies, he found that his respondents, in seeking help for burnout, were least likely to talk to their boss or their Human Resources team. Speaking with a friend or mental health professional was higher on their radar, however. They didn't really get into the reason why, but perhaps it is because when we speak to a boss or someone with a vested interest in our performance at work, they will guide us automatically to solutions. Worse, often they will even convince us that things are better than they are. This is known as *Toxic Positivity*. It is when someone we talk to doesn't really want to hear that we are not feeling great because, in a way, it brings them down. They want to help, and there is nothing wrong with that, but most people in life don't know that we should take our time over a mental health dip, and the more we try to rush out of it, the more it hangs around. Some problems need time to work through, just as a bad haircut needs to grow itself out! Good management training is to listen and understand first, before listening to solve. If we, as a manager or friend, give the other person the space to breathe and express themselves, it might take some time, but they often find their own way out.

This is not necessarily management training, but a life skill in friendship. Hard to do, especially when someone is suffering.

## So, is it us or is it them?

The causes of burnout could be within you, or they could result from a toxic environment. It could be a blend of both. It will vary from situation to situation, and person to person. I hope if you are a manager, you will be aware of the needs of employees, and the environments which can breed burnout culture. If you are an employee, my wish is that you think about the needs you have from your manager/boss/team/workplace, as well as considering your human frailties, which we discussed in the previous chapter, that might lead you up that ladder.

# CHAPTER 4
# THE BURNOUT LADDER®
# AND HOW TO AVOID IT

## The Burnout Ladder®

How do you feel about going up ladders? We have a lot of them in life, both physical and metaphorical. We go up ladders to get somewhere, like a roof or an attic space, or to reach the ceiling that we are trying to paint. Perhaps, our lives are just one big ladder. It is sometimes called the 'career ladder of success.' We talk in our vernacular of 'going up in the world' and of people as 'social climbers.' Each rung of the ladder is a step towards something greater than before, towards our own self-improvement and growth. The problem with ladders is that going up can be perilous if we don't have the right equipment or safety precautions. It's just as easy to fall off as it is to ascend. We have to make sure we get on the right ladder, or we could suffer a nasty fall. What if you thought you were climbing a ladder of success, but all the time it was burning under you? On this specific ascent, there are a series of rungs you step on to, but what you don't realise as you progress, is that the ladder you are climbing is starting to catch fire. The flames are licking around your feet. If you don't see it or feel it, then you may not be aware that, as you keep going, you are getting inexorably closer to the fall. As the ladder collapses, you land in a pile of ashes. This is called The Burnout Ladder®.

I developed The Burnout Ladder® as a framework to understand what is happening as the ascent unfolds. Each rung is a stage of burnout, having its own set of symptoms and watchouts. Burnout creeps up on us, and takes us over, so much so that we lose orientation of ourselves. Have you ever ascended stairs or a ladder, and then looking down, become amazed at how far above the ground you now are? It is easy to lose touch with where we are and need some signposts. That is the first step, to determine our current position, but then we need to know how to get off The Burnout Ladder®. *It is not the one you should be climbing.* There are other ones you can get on to which will be far better for you. (I am writing that book next!) What's more, notice I said you would 'land in a pile of ashes', not 'you are a pile of ashes.' Remember the optimism of the Dostoevsky quote from the introduction. We get afraid of burnout. I certainly know I do. Being burned literally is one of my biggest fears. The term itself feels so final and is very emotive. But this kind of burnout is not final–there is a way back. That said, it is generally better to prevent a problem rather than to cure it.

Each rung of the ladder has its own tool bag of techniques to get you back up to the top, and perhaps off the cursed thing altogether. I work with companies and individuals to equip them with the necessary artillery to keep them mentally healthy and enjoying an acceptable work-life balance. It eludes so many of us. If you use this book, then you don't need to climb that ladder, but if you do, it is a guide to safety.

## How to use The Burnout Ladder®

The Burnout Ladder® is a process you might say that you would go through, but not one you have to follow in sequence. If you are climbing the ladder, there is no week one to week six or anything like that. You simply see where you are and work on the tools to get you off that ladder to safety. If you take the assessment on my website, then you should have a good idea where you might be on the ladder. You can focus there if you want to, but I do recommend reading all the stages, since you may recognise other symptoms that you have already experienced or watch out for others further up.

The ladder consists of six ascending rungs, as in the diagram below (Figure 2).

We start climbing from the bottom rung obviously. The flames won't be alight when you get on the ladder, but the kindling may already be in place. Here are the rungs of the ladder that we follow in sequence.

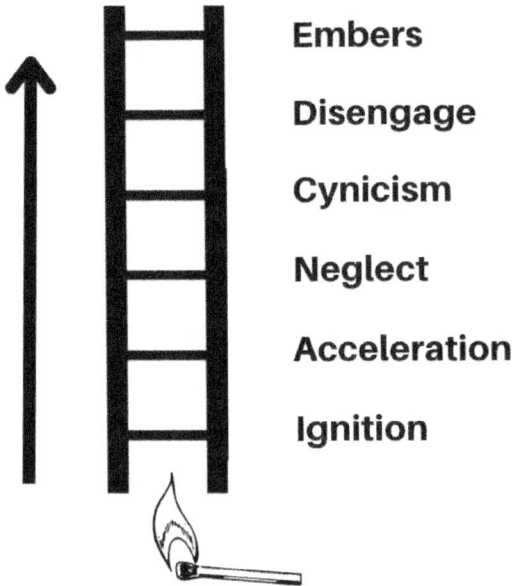

*Figure 2. The Burnout Ladder® with the stages or rungs of burnout.*

1. **Ignition:** An initial decision or action, whether voluntary or involuntary to increase your workload or up the pace at work. Usually a period of excitement and perhaps trepidation or nerves. This is a dangerous and enticing stage, but the only rung of the ladder we should be on. It's exciting too, which is its allure.

2. **Acceleration:** When the impact of the extra work happens—a period of adrenaline rush.

There may be intrinsic rewards for going fast and learning new skills. But just as we feel the buzz of progress, some negativity rears up too.

3. **Neglect:** The beginnings of classic signs of burnout, when we sacrifice our own needs and those of others to maintain the pace. Mistakes start to creep in, which can cause us anguish. We are starting to look tired and drawn.

4. **Cynicism:** The initial highs have gone, and now we are resenting the time and energy spent on work. We are missing hobbies and key family moments. Stress makes us irritable, and we may escape into unhealthy activities for respite from the pressure and grind. We start to doubt our own ability to get through this.

5. **Disengage:** Active social withdrawal and cognitive impairment setting in, lacking care or passion for ourselves or anyone much. We dislike the job we are doing intensely. Struggling to concentrate. Still working hard but not functioning so well, focusing on events we cannot control.

6. **Embers:** Given up, shutting down and becoming dysfunctional, feeling of helplessness and being socially isolated. Sleep is of poor quality, and we haven't any get-up-and-go to do what we love. This is the final stage before burning out.

This looks a lot like symptoms of depression. The burning ladder is just about to collapse...

## It's hard to see the danger signals when the carrot is dangled

Burnout creeps up on us and grabs us because there are so many seductive elements along the way. It seems counter-intuitive, but think of the poor imaginary frog, enjoying itself in cool water in a pot when gradually, the heat is turned up, and then it's too late. We too, might be enjoying a metaphorical swim before realising the water is hotting up. We can be lured in by the human need to be needed, and flattered that extra work is given to us. Sometimes praise is lavished upon us by a wily and skilled manager. We get pulled in, intoxicated with the rewards, even if we feel that we have no choice but to work harder. Nobody wants to feel the effects of burnout, just as nobody wants to become morbidly obese after eating a hamburger and fries daily. In a sense, the same thing happens. As humans, we prioritise an immediate reward over the risk of long-term penalty. It's not today's hamburger that piles on the weight; it's a succession of them. It is not this all-nighter I am pulling to get this presentation done to meet my boss's deadline, it is the weeks/months of that behaviour. Working hard to deliver a result can give us a mental boost, especially if we are recognised and praised for the effort. That gives a little nudge in the reward pathways in the brain, and a mental note is made to do that again and again.

At the early stages, those negative biases we talked

about as mind traps in Chapter 2: Causes of Burnout are less obvious, or if we are aware of them, we use them as a motivator, not a blocker.

## The need to impress

Reward is one lookout. The other main one for me is that, since we are tribal by ancestry, we have a need to impress others and be accepted in our community. Our need to show others that we are pleasing them drives us to forget our own personal boundaries and go above and beyond. We have a need to fit into the crowd. Our primitive brains of 50,000 years ago might reason that we risked being ostracised and not getting access to resources (basic ones such as food and heat) if we didn't pull our weight. This, back in palaeolithic times, was an existential threat. We may not want to be the chief or the shaman, but we don't want to be the oik who nobody likes. Hence our anxiety about keeping up with the pack and getting a buzz out of praise for a job well done. The mind wants to keep getting the reward of recognition and will provide a feel-good boost to motivate you to keep doing it. It is the 'keep doing it' which becomes a trend in behaviour and leads to a quick ascent up the ladder.

## How you can look for signs of burnout

In each stage of the ladder throughout this book, there are typical **symptoms**—this is something you are experiencing and can possibly consider factual. Such as palpable excitement and butterflies in your stomach at being told you have been promoted, or a tight feeling in your chest at how you will cope now that someone has gone on maternity leave and you think your mother is starting to suffer from dementia.

There are also **Watch-Outs**, which, in this book, are something slightly less tangible than symptoms. They are not something that is happening to you as such but could be drivers of your behaviour. They are threats which are appearing on your horizon. An example of this is something you might think or predict at the start of your journey—unrealistic expectations about your capacity to cope with the work you are doing. You don't know yet if you can do it or not, but you have made a prediction that you can. It's not happened yet. Another might be that you have a need to show your status and annoy the hell out of someone in the office who has always lauded it over you with their apparently superior knowledge. How nice it would be to get that promotion and have them working for you! You see the difference? It's not something that is happening, like exhaustion or resentment, a physical symptom, but a thought, feeling, or future threat which will guide your next actions. It is usually poor thinking that drives us into unsustainable and unhealthy behaviours.

Anyway, don't get too hung up on the difference between symptoms and watch outs. I have listed them in a separate section at the back of the book, and if you see them or feel them in yourself, then you follow the next step, which is to choose the tools that will prevent you from climbing further up the ladder. To do that you will need to refer to the appropriate chapter to get the instructions.

## Is The Burnout Ladder® too reactive to the problem?

This observation has been made and, in my view, you definitely shouldn't wait until you feel like you are going to burn out before you adopt these tools and behaviours. They can all be applied, even if you are feeling on top of the world and in full control of your life. I ask you, though, who is? The point of burnout is that it is like a silent killer. You have a smoke or carbon monoxide alarm at home, and you test it regularly and frequently, of course. If the test shows it doesn't work, you change the batteries or fix the wiring. It's nobody's fault, nothing has gone wrong, but we all need our batteries changed or recharged at times. Even if you don't feel at risk from burnout, you can routinely check yourself and see if all is well. Getting into good habits and using these tools is like (and I know this is a cliché now) going to a mental gym. You would not expect to eat badly, hardly take any exercise, and expect to have your body in great shape. It is the same for the mind. Keep it toned, and it will steer you through the tough times.

If you feel you are experiencing any of the symptoms of this book, then it is wise to look at the tools and use them—the ones you like that resonate with you, as not everything will. If you find it works as a strategy, then keep using them, build them into your habits, and look at the next ones you like. Change is daunting and ineffective when we try and take on too much at once. Slow and steady wins the race; the hare and the tortoise, and all that ...

Note that I only use the tools *once* to correspond with a particular step on the ladder, because they are *the most appropriate* at that stage, but that doesn't mean you can't use them anywhere and anytime. I advocate getting good quality sleep when you are at the final Embers stage of the ladder, about to fall into the ashes, but of course, I recommend getting a good night's sleep every night! It will help prevent you from climbing this cursed ladder! Same goes for regular exercise. Just moving and doing something is fantastic for our mental health. I would not wait until you really feel you're at the Neglect phase of the burnout journey to do some physical activity. If I were sharing a PowerPoint presentation now, I would show you a graphic of a temple, and in the foundations would be Exercise, Sleep, and Diet. Non-negotiable. They should be, but often are not, prioritised. If you find yourself at a particular rung of the ladder, and you see one of these as a potential remedy for you, then it is as well to be paying attention to that as a priority.

And this is the kicker; life gets busy. We forget to do the things which are good for us, especially when endlessly treading the hamster wheel, so if this book reminds you to do the activities you know work for you at any stage, then just do it.

# How to use this book

In this workbook, there are pieces to read, and exercises to complete. Some of them may be quick, others should be almost daily or whenever you need them. Keep this manual as your constant companion—on your desk, and the first thing you pack into your laptop bag when you go to the office or on a work trip (after your laptop and power chord obviously). It will help you step down the ladder, step off it altogether, and hopefully prevent you from getting on it in the first place.

In each rung of the ladder, I will identify certain symptoms most commonly associated with each stage of the journey to burnout. This can be a quick eyeball check for you to see if this stage of the ladder is relevant to you or not. Firstly, a disclaimer: we are not all the same, and we experience situations in different ways. We all come at problems from different angles and leave them with different preferences and solutions.

In the next chapter, I have included a link to a questionnaire which will help you to decide if you feel you are burning out and at what stage of The Burnout Ladder® you may be at. If you don't wish to take that, then you can review the symptoms and watch-outs identified in the Appendix. Sitting alongside them are the tools I recommend most appropriately for that rung. You could then jump to that chapter directly if you wish. That said, as stated earlier, you might miss some important background on other stages yet to be encountered if you don't read all the book!

If you like what you read and most importantly,

trying out the tools for yourself, then by all means, contact me for more information on courses and programmes. I would love to hear your feedback, as I am always looking to improve what I can offer for burnout sufferers.

# CHAPTER 5
# THE BURNOUT
# QUESTIONNAIRE

## Am I burning out, or aren't I?

You may well have skipped to this chapter, I know. Especially if you are worn out and just want to know where the hell you might be in your burnout journey, or if indeed you are at risk at all. If you have arrived at this page directly, then I do recommend you read the rest of the book or at least the chapter on The Burnout Ladder® before this one, where I explain the basics behind the six stages, or rungs, of burnout. If not, then there is no harm whatsoever in going ahead and just completing the assessment here. You will need to have some guidance on how to interpret the result, however, and access to the tools I prescribe. It's all in this book; there is no missing treasure, but I intended the chapters to be a story to tell as to why we get into trouble and how to get ourselves out again.

Remember that burnout is like the carbon monoxide of workplace illnesses. You never quite know it's happening to you until deep into the process. So you could be either burning out, burned out already, or just about to move one rung up the ladder.

The six rungs of the ladder provide a climb towards burnout, and the assessment tool (questionnaire) is designed to pinpoint exactly where you are, so that you may navigate your escape more effectively. If you have one particular score which sticks out above the others, then you may head directly to that 'rung', of course, if that is your preference. Sometimes it is not so clear cut, and you may need guidance in reviewing the results, or just read all the information that may be pertinent.

The questions have been devised from my own experiences, a lot of reading, and from talking to burnout sufferers. I have road tested the assessment and am satisfied that it gives a really good starting point for an awareness of the syndrome. One client said, *'it wasn't so much the score but the questions I was being asked which didn't half make me think! I could start to recognise where I was on the ladder from the way I was answering them.'*

There may feel as if there is some duplication between the rungs of the ladder, but this is deliberate as there is naturally some blurring of boundaries between stages, and another reason why self diagnosis is difficult to achieve. We don't just say, 'right, I think I am ready for Neglect stage now.' Life is not always so simple and we don't always have flashing beacons, or an 'X' that marks the spot.

All you have to do is simply go through the 60

questions and answer as truthfully as you can with respect to the way you are feeling right now. Don't think too much about the answers, you don't need to be precise, as we are talking rough direction here. The magic, or perhaps not so magic, number is 25 for each rung of the ladder. Anything above this is worthy of deeper study for that particular burnout stage. So you could start there if you are pushed for time and focus on that chapter, although I do recommend if you have got this far, pushing on and reading all of them. For example, if you are at the Cynicism rung in your score, then you might recognise some of the earlier symptoms of Acceleration, and this might stand you in good stead if you ever go back there. You might also get a warning as to what is to come in the later rungs, so that you can nip those symptoms in the bud.

The assessment doesn't take long and you will get some real insight into your own behaviours and thinking at this time. If you have any concerns over the results then drop me an email and I can provide further assistance, or get some useful tips from www. theburnoutladder.com

Scan this QR code to go to the assessment.

# CHAPTER 6
# RUNG 1: IGNITION

Sometimes you feel you have no choice but to work harder than you do. Ends must be met and extra money found to make it all worthwhile. There is no doubt that it is getting tougher to achieve the same standard of living as we were enjoying just over a decade ago. The average weekly wage in the UK is 8% lower than it was in 2008 after adjusting for inflation (Ref. 15). Many of us simply cannot afford to turn work down. It can feel as if we *must* get an additional income or go for that promotion at work. There are those who have other commitments such as caring for a family or a sick relative, partner, or friend, as well as holding down a full-time job. If you fall into this category, you are, I hope, the exception, and that it should not be for a long period in your life that you are struggling through this.

This is the first rung of The Burnout Ladder®. I agonised over what to call this stage because we come at this from so many different angles. I called it IGNITION because this is when a decision is made to actively make a change, however small or large, in working conditions. It's a little like turning the key in your car, or nowadays, pressing a button. There is a decision point to go, and as you execute, all systems get ready for action. It may also feel like a fire is being lit, because it is a period of excitement as well as trepidation. I originally called this the Decision phase, but recall from Dr. Maslach's causes list in Chapter 3: The Toxic Workplace that burnout can also come from the result of a toxic environment over which we have little or no control. In theory, you could argue that everything is a personal choice. Many self-help books will advocate that whatever happens to us from external forces, we always have a choice in what we think or do. While I am a big proponent of choosing a positive attitude as a way to fend off a negative one, circumstances in life are heaped upon us to a large degree, and so we must deal with that. We are at the mercy of expectations from others, keeping up with the Jones's, victims of unfortunate health circumstances of our nearest and dearest. And at the heart of it lies our innate human traits of competitiveness, overcoming challenge, need for progression, job satisfaction, and self-fulfilment. We need to grow. We need to hit goals in life. It's too high-handed to be judgmental about the choices we make. That said, we can always get better about our responses to those choices. If we are going to accept the challenges, we need the skills and tools to be able to handle that. We will discuss more of that later. For now, let's be kind to ourselves. It sometimes feels as if we don't have any other options but to get sucked in and do more. We progress along with the juggernaut of life.

If you do make an active choice about working harder or longer or both, it doesn't mean you should neglect your own needs, and there are tools and activities throughout this book which will help you at any stage of life, whether at risk of burnout or not. This chapter is designed to give you the chance to think about what your motives are for change. What are you about? Why are you driven to do the things you do? What really makes you tick and guides your actions? This is a huge topic, and probably a book in and of itself. At this rung of the ladder, before the fire gets burning, there is some time to sit back and think about what is important to you in life. The tools in this section are geared towards reflection rather than action. The carpenter's mantra is to measure twice and cut once. I will twist that somewhat and ask you to look twice before you get on this ladder. There are others you could climb if you need to!

So why do you want that promotion? Why do you feel you need to volunteer for that project, or organise that employee conference? Unfortunately, there is usually more than one answer, confusing the mind and its motives. There are causes and symptoms here, as some motives which appear on the surface may not be the primal driving need. For example, the most obvious motivation is to earn extra cash, which none of us would turn down if it fell in our laps. But underneath, somewhere deep inside, we know that for every pay rise we ever get, within a few weeks or months, it is as though we never got one. Our standard of living adjusts to the money we earn very quickly, and once we have got our first job, each rise is incremental rather than life-changing. It is rare, therefore, that it is purely the money which is the motivator. Often, it is the need for status which lights the fire inside, and how we look to others. We might want to demonstrate our prowess within our peer friend group or to our partner, or to the irritating oiks in our teams that don't have our talent but are awfully good at managing upwards. It makes us feel good inside to know that our career is moving on rather than stagnating, and also to have others know we are doing well too.

This is not a bad thing to be in this position. This book is not about quelling ambition. I am simply asking you, on this rung, to step back and examine your own motives and be honest with yourself. Is the game worth the candle? Where is your personal journey (not anybody else's) taking you? And does this next move take you in that direction, or at least not too far from your path? Because, unless you are true to yourself, and are authentic in your actions, you will suffer in the long run. You need to know your *why*. And that is the reason the tools in this section are largely about looking into our own needs and desires.

## The need for challenge

We need new challenges as human beings, as we become bored and less productive if we don't move on. If you're reading this book, you are likely to be working on something much more sophisticated and involving higher stakes than your first ever day at work. You are probably infinitely more skilled in your current role than you were the day you took it on. Those early tasks, once mastered, meant you could move on to others. There have been times when you felt you bit off more than you could chew, maybe technically or intellectually, and you felt overwhelmed at first. But this was part of the growing pains. The more you challenge yourself, the faster and bigger you will grow.

## Go with the flow

Have you ever felt that utter absorption in a task, where the thing itself was its own reward, and everything external to that was blocked out? It is a wonderful state to be in, simply because it allows us to be in the moment; feel as if we are in control of what we are doing and not worry about anything outside of that. The recognition of this psychological state came from the Hungarian/American psychologist Mihaly Csikszentmihalyi (Ref. 16), who found that when individuals were in this position, they would be at their most creative, productive, and content. The most effective way to get into flow state is to do something where your ability to do it is matched by the level of difficulty. If you look at Figure 3, you will see that there is a sweet spot for us between being overwhelmed and anxious on the one hand and bored on the other. If capability matches challenge, then we find a flow state and a contentment in the task. This usually applies to fun activities such as our hobbies but can be applied to any chore or work function too.

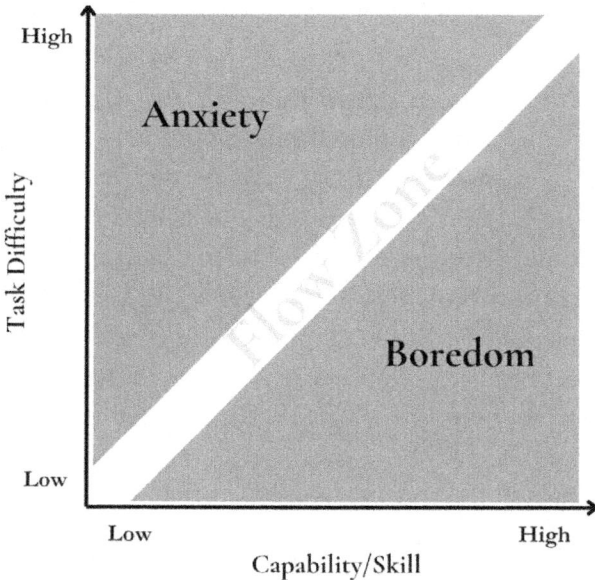

*Figure 3. Flow Zone diagram—based on the work of Mihaly Csikszentmihalyi*

It also demonstrates why we get bored once we have mastered something, and why we continually have to 'up' the challenge as our ability increases. Imagine throwing a ball in the air repeatedly and then catching it. Probably, you would be in the 'Flow Zone' for about two throws. Then, you would be too good for the task, and you would move out of Flow Zone and into Boredom. Then, you decide to up your challenge and try to juggle five balls, and if you don't have any experience or any tuition, they would probably all come crashing down in just a few seconds, which would leapfrog you over the Flow Zone and into Anxiety!

If you are an accomplished juggler, and can handle,

three balls comfortably, then you might find yourself in the Flow Zone. Your skill matches the difficulty of the task, but it is still something which requires concentration and focus. What is more, you find yourself in almost a state of bliss or trance. This is when time can have no meaning and you can just 'be' in the moment you are in. After a while, as you become more accomplished, you will veer towards the right of the chart again, as your skill outperforms the difficulty, so you become bored. The brain seeks novelty and challenge, so you add a ball and make it four. For a short time, you will be positioned suddenly on the left of the chart as the difficulty is greater than your skill. As you rise to the task, you will then go back into the Flow Zone. Something is either too easy or too hard, so you will be adding balls to juggle or take them away. In burnout, we tend to just add them, and one major reason that we do that is because we have ended up on the bottom right on the chart and need to be stimulated once again. We need to ignite a flame and get motivated.

If we consider what it's like to start a job and then move through the various stages of competence and difficulty, it could look something like Figure 4 below. Starting on the bottom left of the chart, we would typically move through this see-sawing journey of Flow, Boredom, and Anxiety.

Here is what the plotted path looks like and why it can happen this way:

0.  **Starting out: often known as** *unconscious in-competence* as we haven't a clue yet what we do

not know. There will be some anxiety (as well as the halo glow of the 'honeymoon period').

1. **Getting the hang of it:** Moving from low difficulty/low capability; this is also unconscious incompetence too. We need to walk before we run, so we are not taking on all the most difficult aspects at this stage. Yet, we have achieved some early wins and feel like we are rising to the challenge.

2. **Increasing difficulty as we take on more and develop the role:** Our capability and capacity match it, so all is good. Still Flow-ing.

3. **Getting too good for it, some boredom:** We appear to be mastering the role and its difficulty has levelled off. We need more challenge.

4. **Sudden step up in difficulty/volume:** Back into anxiety and potential burnout risk if we stay here. It is not so much the task difficulty sometimes, but the volume, the stress, or the sheer frustration at not being able to get what we need to over the line through no real fault of our own.

5. **Reduced efficacy:** As we start to burn out our effectiveness is reduced, leading to deeper anxiety.

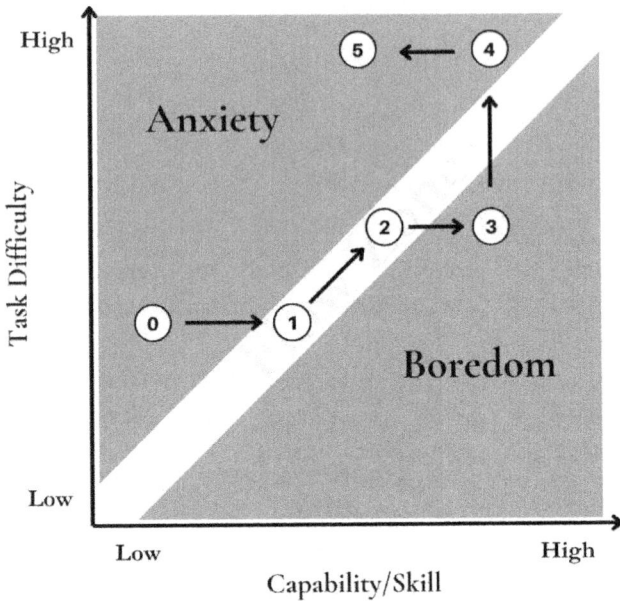

*Figure 4. A path to burnout*

## Meeting the need of reward

We all have needs and are ultimately driven by the reward of meeting them. We may chuckle patronisingly at a dog that behaves well in order to get treats, but our complex brains are actually just the same. We are astonishingly simple and predictable creatures. To ensure our survival, we have a mechanism that encourages us to repeat certain actions which reward us. We have what the neuroscientists call 'reward pathways' in our brain, which are helped along by a neurotransmitter called *dopamine* (a neurotransmitter is a chemical in the brain that can either speed up or inhibit the electrical signals which flash across the brain as we make neural connections). This acts as a kind of marker when something happens that is good, thus giving you the reminder to do it again, a little blip of feel-good factor. Dopamine was very useful to our hunter-gatherer ancestors if they saw a bush full of berries to eat, and their brains gave them a rewarding boost as a result, for the next action is to eat those berries and avoid starvation. Like the dog, the brain ensures we continue to get our treats, and a friendly pat on the head for finding the bush in the first place. This reward system ultimately powers us in everything we do, from gaming on our phones, to smoking a sly cigarette. If the reward is there, we just do it, as it is an immediate buzz. This is why it is so hard to kick bad habits which give us pleasure immediately. The reward we get from watching Netflix on the sofa is more powerful than the immediate pain derived from putting on running shoes and putting ourselves through a 5 km run, so defaulting to watching TV often wins out. The long-term gain of taking the exercise is clearly better for us, but the brain likes quick wins. (For a fully comprehensive and effective view on how to kick bad habits and start new and better ones, I recommend James Clear's work on *Atomic Habits*, a best-selling book on Amazon.)

When it comes to our incentives for working harder, our main motive for working harder is usually for more cash. That might be to cover the utilities bill or go towards a dream holiday. As you read on, I will ask you to think about what your motives might be. This is not to challenge you, dissuade you, or make you feel guilty for having material desires like wanting a new car. You have needs, and your brain will want them to be met. To consider what is driving those needs at this stage will be useful. If you are heading on that burnout journey, this is where you get on to the ladder, and it's vital to know what is encouraging the first step up to make sure your rewards will be consistent with your personal values.

Imagine your boss asks you to step up to cover a senior role suddenly vacated. They may play all the tunes about how this will be good for you, and that it is a challenge, it will look good for your profile, how much you will learn. You are more likely to be in line for promotion next time around if you help them out now. I have been here, when I was asked to cover for a director who had left the company just before a major systems go-live, which ultimately proved highly disruptive (a.k.a. disastrous) to the business. Thoughts that went through my mind were:

'This will up my profile.'
'This experience will look good on my CV.'
'I might get the job proper if it comes up.' (I didn't)
'Scared. Can I do it?'
'Hours might be crazy.'
'Can I get another job if I fail?'

There was no extra cash on the table, but I thought I had better do it. My motives for wanting to look good were classical, as were my doubts on the other side of the coin, but the truth is, I was deciding mostly out of fear. Even the more positive thoughts of 'this will look good or improve me' were based on a primal terror that if I didn't step up, then I would be falling behind. Grow or die. The context was that I had emigrated from the UK to Canada less than a year earlier. I was, for the large part, trading on some specific industry trend know-how that I had gleaned in the UK that was now becoming fashionable in North America. My self-confidence, although not low, was not as high as it could have been because I was in a state of overwhelm, having immigrated to a new country and making my way in a senior management role for a major blue-chip company. I was still on the Anxiety side of the Flow Zone. This influenced me greatly, because I felt that if I rejected the proposal, then I might be black-marked. On the other hand, one part of my brain was titillated and flattered! I thought this might be my major break, and a door had opened up for me which might not happen again (fear). The factors I didn't consider were that if I said 'no,' then I might get respect for standing my ground. My UK knowledge would surely have given me some leverage to find another role if it came to that. If I had been brave enough to up sticks and move continents, then surely I must have the gumption to get another job and survive. I wasn't thinking like that at the time, however. Sometimes we only see the next pay cheque, and vision is blurred by doubt.

Looking back, though, I am glad I took on the challenge. Regret what we've done, not what we've *not* done, goes the old saying. The experience grew and stretched me, and I got a great end-of-year performance review and grade. Again, to avoid The Burnout Ladder® doesn't mean stifling ambition, but I didn't have the necessary tools to keep me healthy. If you use those that I am offering up in this book, then there's no reason why your ladder needs to burn.

The way our minds work in such circumstances is complicated, and my thinking was more intuitive than structured, as well as being very tactical as opposed to strategic. I suggest that if you are at this Ignition rung of the ladder, that you take a step back to consider your motives for taking on extra work. If the move is consistent with your own needs and values, then it seems logical to just go for it. Having the awareness of doing so, before you decide, is vital for me though. Everyone is different (and who am I to judge you), but if you are acting when it is not really in *your* interests to do so, then that way leads to trouble in the long term. Also, when you consider this, think about whether you are acting out of fear or reward. Will the extra effort reward you and make you feel good, or are you doing it to avoid feeling bad? I think I was in the latter camp, and I am not sure it helped me, because somewhere deep down, my confidence wasn't there, and that's the wrong way to kick off. We must remember to be consistent with our own 'why'. If we don't, our lack of authenticity will find us out.

I am playing Dr. Frankenstein with rewards and motives, and as such, I have created a table below based on human needs work adapted and moulded from two separate sources (Dr. Abraham Maslow and his

Hierarchy of Needs (Ref. 10), and Dr. Richard Hanson from his book *Resilience* (Ref. 17). The principle is that we need to satisfy certain needs in life. Some are basic survival, some are grander, and of course, not everyone will have the same goals. I would like you to take a few moments to do this exercise, so that you may consider what your motives are in life. That does sound very highfalutin, and maybe not something you should just scribble down while you are having a cup of coffee, but even just a few minutes work and thinking here will give you some insights into what it is you are looking for. It will give you something to measure your current decisions against.

## Motives, self-awareness, and looking out for burnout traps

The table is designed, as per the Hierarchy of Needs, to go from bottom to top in terms of what you need to satisfy in your own life. Our first need, as with any other animal, is to provide a foundation for life by achieving **Safety**. This is a fear-based need. We might fear being attacked or killed by a predator, or the lack of basic resources such as food and shelter. This means having a secure roof over our heads and enough calories to keep us going through the day. These elements are fundamental rights as a living animal, and the absence of them causes huge anxiety of course. It is why we get a job in the first instance: to have a home to live in and to buy food. In a cruel twist of mental manipulation, we also tend to think this need is at risk far more than is necessary. Following this logic has not been uncommon for me. Example: things are not going well on this project > I might be viewed as incompetent > I might get managed out of the business > I may not get another job > I could be homeless ... Therefore, I double down on effort and work extra hard, just to fulfil this basic need, at least in my own head.

The next need is that of **Satisfaction**. This is reward-based. Like it or not, we all live based on rewards; for that little dopamine high which keeps us repeating an activity. This is when we feel good after finding that bush full of berries, so that we might be motivated to find more of them and feel satisfied rather than just safe. We are like dolphins at the pool show, leaping up and performing tricks so we can be fed treats of fish. The fish provide the satisfaction and the motivation to keep showing up. This is where life gets more fun. Being able to afford more meals out, flashier holidays, good theatre tickets. We only get to here after we have met the requirements of Safety.

We are wired for **Connection** to others. We are herd animals and as such, we need to cooperate, feel loved, give love, feel useful and look it too. Be careful of the trap of doing things just to impress others, as it will lead you away from your own values. Looking for the perfect holiday snap to post on social media is one such example. Why do we do this? Why do we need others to see we are doing well? We need to be seen as having status so that we will not be ostracized and cast aside as useless. It's a primal tribal need for connection. We have a pride, therefore, in doing well and being seen to be doing well, even if underneath, we are struggling like hell. That is one major predictor of burnout: performing for others, and yet, when it all boils down to it, a harsh reality exists. *We care more about what they think of us, than they actually think of us.*

If we achieve all the above, then we shoot for **Self-fulfilment**, or self-actualisation as Dr. Maslow put it. That means achieving longer term goals, such as becoming a pillar of the community, a loving parent, publishing a book, leaving a legacy. This can mean different things to different people. It might mean having a flashy car and house, way beyond the simple need of just being satisfied with what you have. It could be that you want to give your money away to a charity because of your philanthropic leaning. These motives will almost certainly drive a burnout risk. Such people are driven, and are often perfectionists (more on that in the next paragraphs). They also tend to be somewhat paranoid that they are not doing enough, and that what they have achieved and what they have earned is not enough. It could leave them unable to enjoy and celebrate current successes, because they have to be off achieving the next big thing.

If you look at the bracketed words by each stage in the table on pages 87–88, they give you a simple view of how we are psychologically wired to behave or act. Starting with Safety—this is fear-based—the need to simply survive driven by a primal fear of not doing so. We are avoiding the lack of safety. Satisfaction is reward-based. Having ensured survival for the time being (none of us will be here forever), we can tap into reward systems by doing things we like. We are approaching fun things that make us feel good about who we are and the time we are having on Earth. Connection is a fundamental human requirement. It is something we need to do to enhance our survival and satisfaction status. Finally, self-fulfilment is the crowning glory of it all, when we feel we have made it in life.

I don't want to make this complicated. I developed this table just to make you aware of what is driving you *now*, and make you think about your own needs and some of the traps you might fall into. Again, awareness is all. It's just a thought-jogger. Are there traps associated with your needs and desires?

## Burnout traps

In Chapter 2: Causes of Burnout, we discussed human mind traps relating to burnout. In a sense, these are similar, or at least driven from those primal needs. In the table, there are columns for our human needs and the burnout traps which could arise as a result. Again, it is entirely subjective as to whether they are good or bad for you. But they are considerations and motivations, and they will have a huge part to play in driving you.

## Characteristics which lead us into burnout traps

**Material needs:** The basic motivation for working.

I don't know if it is some kind of maxim or law, but however much we earn, we tend to spend it, just as gas expands to fill whatever space it inhabits. If our income is increased, is life any better—really—afterwards? We may be working harder, holding down two jobs even, just to make ends meet or get the best life possible for our children. Feeding a family isn't a trap, it's a necessity and a duty. But it can be road to burnout if you are doing too much for something you don't need.

**Perception:** We spend an awful lot of time guessing at what others think of us. And how often do we find that we get it wrong? If we feel that we will be negatively judged because we turned down an opportunity for a promotion, or that we are defending our work boundaries by not taking on more, it is only a feeling, not a fact. And, if indeed the perception is correct, is that more important than our own self-worth?

**Excitement:** Don't we love it? Don't we get bored when things just tick along? We thrive on adrenaline sometimes, for short amounts of time at least, and the prospect of an exciting role, which may be beyond our capability right now, is exactly what the prospect of Flow Zone is all about: the challenge to get better.

**Impressing others:** The need for status, to show our peers that we are doing well, is quite natural within a tribe. Why else are we so competitive by nature? It drives us forward to be better. Are we doing whatever we are doing though, because of how we need to look or because it's what we want? This is a really tough one, since there is scarcely any greater joy than the emotion of pride when someone tells us they are impressed with what we have achieved. It is important not to let that become the main driving force. 'Am *I* impressed with *myself*?' is the question to ask.

**Unrealistic expectations of self:** Just how far forward do we really need to go? How perfect do we need to be? To improve at anything, we need to push ourselves. But do we need to push so far? Are we setting ourselves up for a fall by setting impossible targets? Perfectionism drives this, and the disappointment which ensues from falling short is not only damaging in itself, but so are the behaviours which could follow: avoiding challenge because of previously damaging experiences. More to follow in this chapter.

Spend some time doing this activity. Set aside 15 minutes with a mug of something in a quiet place. Investigate your motives for wanting or needing to make a change.

## Are your needs leading you into burnout traps?

Let us imagine you are contemplating a change in work which might lead to increased workload, stress, or pressure. There is no defined pattern as to how you should be. Ask yourself some questions relating to why you are taking on the challenge. Even if it feels you have 'no choice.' I would simply like you to look at the table, paying particular attention to the typical burnout traps associated with each one. Are these the motives that you have? Is there anything you would like to challenge in yourself about the way you are thinking? Above all, be honest with yourself. If you come out saying yes, I bloody well want to work my butt off to get that car, then so be it. Why not? Just go through the process of self-awareness and make your decision conscious, rather than sleepwalking into a nightmare because your subconscious motives weren't aligned to who you really are. Use your notebook, and think with your pen as you use the chart below. What are your motives for taking on this change? There are no right or wrong answers to this one.

| Human Need | Characteristics | Burnout Traps |
|---|---|---|
| SELF-FULFILMENT (realisation, pursuit of perfection) | • Status<br>• Self-Actualisation<br>• Achievement | • High/unreasonable expectations of self<br>• Impressing others<br>• Need for life perfection<br>• Materialism-dream holidays/houses/cars<br>• Feeling behind in life goals |
| CONNECTION (tribal needs) | • Sexual needs<br>• Attachment<br>• Acceptance | • Looking for kudos, how we appear to be doing<br>• Impressing a current or potential partner<br>• Keeping up with friends/peers<br>• Wanting more cash for socialising |

| Human Need | Characteristics | Burnout Traps |
|---|---|---|
| SATISFACTION (reward-based) | • Seeking rewards<br>• Comfort<br>• Self-worth and esteem<br>• Progression, not stagnation | • Excitement at extra challenge<br>• Wanting more cash for entertainment, eating out, better holidays<br>• Increased pride at extra pay/status<br>• Moving forward and growing |
| SAFETY (fear-based) | • Avoid harm<br>• Provide food, warmth, shelter<br>• Protect self and family | • Cash to move to safer housing/neighbourhood<br>• Need to feed and clothe family<br>• Worrying about perception if not stepping up > job security fears |

## Approach and Avoidance

How did you get on? Hopefully the structure of the matrix and the corresponding burnout risks resonated. I put this here, at the beginning of the ladder because it is a considered exercise which might help later on when you suddenly start yelling at yourself, 'Why am I doing this please?!' Also, it might help you learn something about yourself—are you approach (wanting to do something positively), or avoidance (fear of failure) based? The paradox in all of this is that we are more capable of taking on challenges than we think, dependent upon our mindset and the paradigms we create. It is the reality we have created, depending on how the world looks to us. A situation can look scary (one to avoid) or challenging (one to approach and conquer). When we are fear or avoidance based, we get into survival mode, and the brain thinks less rationally and tightens up its creative muscles. We tend to think about where we don't want to go, and curiously, as you will read in the next chapter in a segment about the subconscious mind, we end up going there anyway. When we are approach based, thinking of positive outcomes, where we want to go, then we will naturally align ourselves more to that. What the hell am I saying? Just do it, and to hell with it all? No. I am saying be considered and go through the exercise above and decide on your motives. Two questions:

1. Are your apparent motives aligned to what you really want deep down?
2. Are you thinking out of approach or avoidance? Desire or fear? Thriving or surviving?

Beware here though—if you talk yourself out of avoidance and into approach, you may well go into your new situation with rose-tinted spectacles. This is one of the watch outs I have identified below, typical of this stage of the ladder. Again, I am not telling you *not* to accept your new change. I am asking you to go in eyes wide open and be balanced about your prospects. Neither too afraid, nor too blind.

Now, **this is the only rung of the ladder that you should be reasonably comfortable being on**. You are at the very bottom of it here, perhaps about to embark upon your journey towards burnout, or maybe about to step off altogether into a land of balance and joy. This is the stage where you are at your most aware, and as such, you give yourself the best chance to make good choices. I have a friend who scores high here, but I am not worried about him stepping up the ladder. He is always up for new challenges, but knows the danger of losing himself in the process.

Word of warning: companies want their employees to have high engagement. That's why their Human Resources teams spend so much time on engagement surveys in the workforce. Engaged workers are prime candidates for burnout simply because they care and will go the extra mile again and again. If we are not engaged, that doesn't mean we are not going to burn out, as under-utilisation can drive it just as much.

As in all the chapters and rungs of the ladder, I have included tools which I think are *most* appropriate to *this* stage of the burnout journey. It doesn't mean that you should be excluding anything else which works for your self-care and wellbeing. If you run daily to manage your stress, you wouldn't just stop doing it. In rungs of the ladder further down, I will recommend sleep as a priority, but to be honest, it should always be a general priority in life, as so many health problems are associated with not getting sufficient 'quality' sleep.

So, let's look at the tools you might need on the Ignition rung.

## Ignition Stage Remedies/Tool 1/WOOP

The first tool I recommend is all about making sure that what you do conforms to your own needs and values.

There are workbooks and courses which deal with this kind of topic. Defining your values and needs so that you remain true to yourself can be a lengthy process, but the point behind the tools in this book is that they are generally quite quick to apply, and don't require months of analysis or therapy.

For these reasons, I have incorporated a process to help you decide what you want, with a planning methodology which means you can aim towards that. This is called **Mental Contrasting**, which I will explain in a moment. And for this, I like the **WOOP** process. This delightful acronym stands for Wish, Outcome, Obstacles, and Plan, and it was pioneered by the psychologist Gabrielle Oettingen (Ref. 18).

## Mental Contrasting

This phrase may sound like a torture of some kind, and it sounds like it might be hard work. It's not at all, but it certainly can be fun. It is based on two major factors which can help you define what it is that you want to get out of life, or your day, or even the next hour. Such is its flexibility. Principally, there are two main factors involved in making sure you achieve something. Firstly, you need to imagine what it is that you want. This is definitely the most fun bit, allowing yourself to dare to dream. It could be scoring less than 80 on the golf course if you are a mid-handicapper, winning an art competition or creating a colourful and beautiful paradise garden. This is where you need to permit yourself to think big. If you don't aim high, then you won't fly high either. Research shows that if you can lock in all of those wonderful feelings about your goal, more so than the result, you are more likely to steer yourself towards it. But it's not enough to dream. You need to act as well, and not only that, but to imagine all the barriers and obstacles which might get in the way. This is where you allow your imagination to work in the other direction. What might be the forces opposing you? In golf, it might be your lack of time to practice, or insufficient tuition and experience with oil paints if you want to win the art competition. It could be that the weather this year is stacked against you and might prevent you from creating horticultural heaven.

Oettingen found that you need both, the Jekyll and Hyde aspects of yourself, if you will. If you just dream then you probably will give up at the first hint of trouble, and if you just think of all the reasons why you won't do something, then you will get discouraged and never start.

## The WOOP process

No self-help or well-being manual would be complete, in my view, without a reference to that icon in this area: Stephen R. Covey, who wrote the timeless classic, *The Seven Habits of Highly Effective People* (Ref. 26). One of his chosen maxims was to 'Begin With the End in Mind.' Back in the 1990s, when this kind of training in the workplace was abundant, this was a phrase we got to use all the time in our office. It is easily forgotten when lost in the weeds. Just where is it we want to go? What is the end goal, the object of all this effort?

This is a highly useful and logical process, combining human skills of imagination and also problem-solving. Starting with the end in mind makes you focus on what you want, to lock you into a future you desire. This gives you the drive to get over all the natural obstacles and issues, which will naturally fall in your way as life encroaches on you. What makes this process so effective is that having imagined the end game, you then dream up those obstacles at the beginning. We don't wait for them to hit us and then scramble to remove them. You will then have a good idea of what they are and be prepared. If it is a marathon you are training for, then potential derailers— time to train, dark cold mornings, the preference to stay in bed, injury worries—all come to mind when you sit down and think about it. You then summon your contingency-planning skills to find alternative paths which will get you round these obstacles.

The process goes much like this:

**Wish**—Sit down and informally just think. What do I want—really want? Don't be specific about goals here (that is the Outcome), but what do I want it to *feel* like. How we feel defines the most important moments in our lives, not how we think. Feeling is something we remember from when we won a school sports day race (or at least didn't drop the baton in the relay), fell in love, became a parent, when our team won the cup, when we lost someone close. Feelings define life. Therefore, be open to your feelings on this exercise. Go and do this sat in the park, or on a walk, or throwing pebbles into the sea. The output of this will be a few words on paper, whatever they may be, but start them with, 'I want to feel…'

**Outcome**—This is where you get more analytical. This is where thinking joins feeling. Having a pretty good idea of what you want, you then define your goal. I have always been a fan of SMART goal-setting (Specific, Measurable, Achievable, Realistic, Timed). Research shows that the less vague we are with our brains, then the less chance it has to wriggle out of the obligation. We generally respond to SMART instructions. If you need to be at work by 8:30 a.m., then you generally are there by that time. That is a specific and timed goal. If your contract said, 'Turn up when you feel like it as long as you get your work done,' then you may start to become more lapse in your timekeeping. State your goals here. 'I will run a marathon in two years' time, and it will be London or Birmingham or New York.' This is specific. It is a defined length of run in a specific place. You can measure it—sure as anything, you will become obsessed over your timing (I have never run a marathon, but anybody I know who has always tells me the time they achieved, without prompting). It is achievable if you set out a training plan and give yourself time to do it. It is realistic if you follow your plan and look after yourself. And of course, it is timed. Not the time you run in, but the time by which you have achieved your goal, in this case in two years' time.

**Obstacle**—What is going to get in your way? What are all the wrinkles you can foresee? List them all down and be exhaustive. You can prioritise and risk-assess later. The key here is to take each of those obstacles and use your imagination to conjure them up.

**Plan**—This is called **Implementation Intention**. That is to say to yourself, 'If… Then …'. For example, IF the weather is too cold in January, THEN I will do some of my marathon training indoors on a treadmill.

There is a certain amount of comfort and confidence taken from the fact that a potential worry, which could fester in your mind and take your energy away, has been addressed and a potential solution found.

**WOOP** is a logical process which you can follow for how you want your day, week, year, or life to be. It also includes your emotions though. How you want to feel. You can write it or just think it out in your head. I do recommend writing it out however, even if just scribbled in your notepad. Just follow the process in the logical order, that's the key. Think of the aim before the obstacles.

Here are some examples which show how versatile this can be:

## EXAMPLE: TODAY

**WISH:** I would really love to feel as if I have accomplished something, however minor, and just actually finish a task!

**OUTCOME:** Specifically, I will finish sowing the

wildflower seeds in the garden, and planting in the borders.

**OBSTACLES:** I am doing a lot of other stuff, like going to yoga this morning and lunching with a friend later. It is possible that I might not have time to do everything. I might also get tired and not have the energy this afternoon to get it all finished. I usually like to work in the mornings.

**PLAN:** If I feel I am running out of time, **then I** will block out just one hour between 4–5 p.m. where I will just work on my must-do-today items.

If I feel I am low on energy, **then I** will drink plenty of water this afternoon to keep me hydrated.

## EXAMPLE: LONGER TERM

**WISH:** I would love to travel around Asia with a backpack, as I never got round to it when I was younger. I want to feel as if I have seen something of the world and meet real local people somewhere, not just hotel staff and tourists in a nice place.

**OUTCOME:** I will travel for three months around Thailand, Cambodia, and Vietnam. I will spend two weeks in Bali at the end of the trip as a relaxing finish before I return to real life. I will do this by the end of 2026.

**OBSTACLES:** I might get ill before I get the chance

to go or feel as if I am too old and not have the energy for the late-night travels or not want to stay in grimy hostels with bed bugs. I might realise that much of travel is boring and stressful, and certainly not as constantly relaxing as being on the beach all day.

**PLAN: If** I feel I am likely to be not fit enough for travelling, **then I** will build a healthy living plan prior to the trip to maximise my fitness and chances of good health.

**If** I am concerned that a lot of travelling may be boring or stressful, **then I** will plan routes so that my travelling between locations is minimised and I can maximise my time absorbed in local culture. I will budget for comfortable and clean accommodation.

**If** it gets boring, **then I** will ensure I have lots of interesting stuff to read on my Kindle while I have downtime; I will level up my relaxation skills and get used to doing very little and just enjoy 'being.' After all, this is half the point of going travelling; to step off the world for a while.

So, the critical steps in this process are:

1. Think and dream big. Because if we don't, then we will always have the edges knocked off our ambition. When we take inputs from others, they usually temper our ambition. Focusing in on the feeling of what it will be like will lock the intention into our subconscious, and our brain will be more motivated to make it happen.

2.  Being specific on the outcome gives the brain a focus for something to work to. We hardly ever execute on such phrases as, 'Oh I wish I could go travelling.'

3.  Identifying and imagining obstacles gives us a sense that we are not just 'pie in the sky.' We are going about our dreams and tasks realistically and professionally. Stuff always gets in the way, that is life, but if we have pre-thought about them, then we won't be blindsided, and we'll be ready with a plan.

4.  The 'If...Then I' planning gives us a sense that we can always find pathways around obstacles. What's more, not everything has to be thought out now. If we spent our whole lives thinking about what could get in the way of our day, we would never get out of bed. We need to trust ourselves that we have done enough thinking and preparation, and that we will use our natural agility to overcome problems.

Why have I put this tool in here? At this stage of the ladder, you are thinking about gearing up for a tougher stint at work, not fulfilling life's dreams. But remember, you can use this process for anything, short-term or long. I encourage you to use the blank lines (page opposite/below) and think about the situation you are in or about to embark upon—your new job, your promotion, covering someone else's tasks. Before you get busy, this is the ideal opportunity to remain strategic about how you approach it. What is it that YOU want? Very often, we are dancing to other's tunes, so take this opportunity to remain in control. How do you want to feel about the work you do? Energised and satisfied, or tired and defeated? Lock in the feeling you want and stay focused on it. You will need other tools to help you do this, but you are setting the intention now, rather than defaulting to burnout. Finally, remember to trust yourself. If things go sideways, you have plans to get round your obstacles. You have pathways and choices, and just being prepared with that thought alone can give you a vital boost of self-confidence.

## What do you want? The WOOP process

Try it for yourself. Either use this space below, or write the headings in your notepad.

### WISH:

_____

_____

### OUTCOME (Specific goals, make them SMART, i.e., Specific, Measurable, Achievable, Realistic, Timed):

_____

_____

### OBSTACLE(S):

_____

_____

**PLAN** (If … Then …):

_____

_____

## Ignition Stage Remedies/Tool 2/Prudent Perfectionism

Perfectionism is something which can drive someone to distraction, as well as those around them. Often, perfectionists are blissfully unaware of the over-exacting standards they place upon others or in the situations they encounter. In the next few pages, we will discuss perfectionism and why it is kryptonite to the burnout sufferer.

The tool of **Prudent Perfectionism** is designed to give you the balance of achieving without driving yourself into the ground, and helping you learn from mistakes along the way, as well as accepting and growing from them.

## When is good—good enough?

In the work I do with mental resilience, I don't major on this topic, but it is important for the topic of burnout. I put it at the base of the ladder because it applies straight away and throughout your perilous climb. If you are the kind of person who tends towards perfectionism, then you need to look at this as a potential cause of your burnout—and you may as well start now, because some habits take a long time to kick.

I am a firm believer in life that 90% will do (mostly). Generally, a lot of natural phenomena follow the Pareto principle, the 80/20 rule. For example, typically, 20% of a company's customers account for 80% of its revenue, so they focus their resources here as it is unviable to apply 'enough' resources to properly look after the 80% majority of customers by volume. The return just isn't there for the income they drive.

Why, then, do some of us choose not to follow this in aspects of our work? How often do we go that extra mile for a triviality which nobody will care about or even remember? Sometimes we don't always have the choice, of course. I had a boss once who was forensically anal about the appearance of PowerPoint slides. I get that we need to look professional and look like we know what we are doing when making presentations, but to ensure that every last font on the title of every slide is exactly matching is absolutely soul-sucking. It is an example of our style-over-substance world. I would far rather be thinking and formulating the content of the story I am telling than worrying about these tiny details. Personally, I think to be 80% right is not quite there, which is why I have (not very scientifically) opted that 90% is good enough. If you were 90% sure of choosing a holiday you are looking at online, you would probably go for it. 80%? You would keep looking. If you needed to be 100% sure, you would never book anything!

Let's look at the different types of perfectionists and what the implications might be to them. Psychologists label them in these three categories:

1. **Self-oriented:** People put pressure on themselves to perform flawlessly.

2. **Other-oriented:** People are held to the highest standards by others (i.e., my PowerPoint-obsessed boss).

3. **Socially prescribed:** Those who feel that they will only get on if they meet the impossible expectations of those around them.

If you are in Category 3 (and think about this for a moment or two), you are, it has been shown, especially prone to stress.

If you hold yourself to high standards, as in Category 1, this is not necessarily a predictor of burnout—unless you *worry* about making mistakes. There is a difference. I can go the extra mile to make sure that this section of the book is perfect, and that's fine. But if I worry that there are mistakes which I don't see but might get picked on, that's where I need to watch out.

We spend far too much time worrying about making mistakes. But if we live or work in a toxic environment, then no wonder. Penalties exist for getting things wrong. We worry about being labelled as calamitous, or we can't be trusted to handle a project. Yet, many company mission statements and value sets talk about being bold and taking risks. Does that mean all risks are expected to come off? No, they won't, of course, and it can be okay unless it impacts someone's bonus, I guess ...

This is a reason why a key tool for this rung is called

*Prudent* **Perfectionism**. Nobody wants to make big howling errors. It's not in our nature to be happy with that. But we do learn from mistakes too. Where is the sweet spot? If you read through the tips, you will see some useful points on adopting a growth mindset—that failure is not necessarily failure, but a pathway to better ways of doing things. Pick your fights too. Some things you can't take risks on because the stakes are too big, which is why you can choose smaller battlefields to test and learn. This means you are judicious about where you spend your time and energy, as you can't give 100% to every aspect of your work and life.

Often, too, we get stressed about starting a task because we want perfection. Just getting going and doing something, even if it's not right yet, is the best way to overcome the perfectionist yips. Correct as you go and apply priorities to decide where you spend your time. If you are an employer, watch your perfectionists. They may be your greatest assets and also your greatest risks for burning out.

In researching perfectionism, I came across a very useful piece of work by Jennifer Kemp, the author of *The ACT Workbook of Perfectionism* (Ref. 19), where she talks about the impacts of this human trait and what it does to us when we don't get things right. She distinguishes between *Helpful* and *Un-helpful* Perfectionism. The helpful type is what makes us strive to be better, using our natural competitive instincts to move forward and achieve the best we can, sometimes driven by the need to compete with others. This is okay, as long as the goals require this, and we can learn to live with making mistakes along the way. Personally, when I get onto an aeroplane, I would like to think that from a safety point of view, an attitude of perfectionism has been prevalent, rather than my '90% will do' philosophy. By making mistakes here, I mean do so in the engineering workshop or as a test pilot ironing out issues, rather than when carrying me on it as a passenger. The safe outcome has probably come from a lot of people doing their job very well, and even then, they are probably not perfect individually, but hopefully the team effort pretty much was.

The other and more concerning variant is Unhelpful Perfectionism, which has further-reaching implications for people over and above just tearing their hair out because they can't get the images aligned on their PowerPoint. Here, she describes another type of inevitable ladder or slide into mental health issues:

It starts with
  a) the need to maintain overly high or ambitious standards,

often driven by
  b) fearing failure or mistakes, or fear of not being liked.

When standards are not met, then we
  c) develop a habit of self-criticism—never feeling good enough.

A consequence of this is
  d) avoidance of reaching for goals because of potential feelings of fear or failure.

And so, generally in life

    e)   making a habit of this trait so it becomes the de facto norm.

So, just as I asked you to consider if you are approach or avoidance-based after the burnout traps table on pages 87–88, this amounts to the same problem. The need to achieve perfect results leads to fear and shrinking away from life's challenges because we feel we won't be good enough. This will likely be self-fulfilling as confidence is eroded, but more importantly, it means we will miss out and live life with more anxiety and fear.

This is an excellent model to explain just what happens to us as perfectionists when we don't hit the mark. If we aim for 100% perfection, there is no room to manoeuvre, and we are likely to be tunnel-visioned by the need to get to where we want to go. If we fall short on that, as is most likely, then we will criticise ourselves. If this voice in our heads starts to get louder, we will shrink away from challenge and start to experience avoidance. In psychology, this means that we will shy away from situations that are likely to provoke feelings of anxiety, yet bizarrely, generate more of it. Our painful memories associated with failure (or self-perceived failure at least), will surface to remind us not to do the same thing again. Thus, we miss out on wonderful opportunities in life to experience and learn, simply because our mindset had set us on this negative spiral, creating a whole lot of angst in the process. This, in step e), becomes the norm for anything we do, not just the thing that we were working on. Avoidance becomes life, and we retreat into our shells and live it non-courageously.

The counter to this is what I call **Prudent Perfectionism**. If you read through to the questionnaire on pages 110–111, you can answer some questions as to whether you might be tending towards unhelpful perfectionism, and then see what you can do about it if you are.

## Getting out of our own way

I play golf a fair bit. I am a mid-handicapper, decent but no Rory McIlroy. I can play well sometimes, and at others, my performance is disappointing (I get disappointed because if I can hit one shot well, then why can't I do that all the time?). There are other factors too. Most of the time I am playing with my pals in some sort of friendly competition. That adds a touch of bite. I don't want to look stupid when I play in front of them. I want to win, to have bragging rights, to make them pay for the bacon butties in the bar afterwards. When I stand over the ball, my overriding thoughts tend to be something like, 'I must make this putt,' or 'I really need to hit this well.' The need for the shot to go well or, let's face it, perfectly, is the very thing that stops it from happening. My muscles tense as I frown in concentration. My arms and legs become locked as my body prepares to strike the ball. The golf swing is a complex and fickle thing, requiring a great deal of mental and physical coordination. It is the mental side that gets in the way. I have swung a golf club thousands of times in my life. My body generally knows what to do and performs well enough most of the time. If I relax mentally, I get out of its way, so to speak, and voila! The ball soars off into the yonder. If I can relax and forget the outcome and just enjoy the process of hitting the ball—it is a pleasurable hobby after all, not a stint on the torture rack—then my muscles are more likely to carry out the task using their own learned behaviour and unconscious memory.

It could happen that the ball flies off roughly in my intended direction and with the right amount of power. The bounce of the ball may be unkind, and it ends up in a bunker by the green. It's not the end of the world. I enjoyed the strike of the ball, and I can get out of bunkers fairly well. If I face other hazards along the way, I know I can navigate them. I need to trust myself and my body that I know what to do and can cope with imperfection and some roadblocks. That's letting go of perfectionism, and if we can apply these principles to life and whatever it is that we are doing, I guarantee results will improve. *We just need to get out of our own way and forget the intended outcome of perfection.*

## Perfectionism and mental health

I want to say here that this is an area of mental well-being that is often overlooked. When someone tells us they can do something for us at the time we want it, we say, "Perfect!"—even if it isn't that amazing, it's just fine, actually. The word creeps into our vocabulary, and so does the need to embody it. Perfectionism is linked with a whole host of debilitating and upsetting illnesses, such as depression, obsessive compulsive disorder, generalised anxiety disorder, social anxiety, panic disorder, and eating disorders, to name but a few. We shouldn't be underestimating this creeping phenomenon, therefore. A simple and obvious example is in body image. The pressure on people nowadays, especially in the young, is to look 'perfect', just like the models, film, and TV stars we see on our screens. People are made fun of because they don't look perfect, and in schools, this kind of shaming is rife. (It always has been, of course, but is made worse by the 24-7 intrusive nature of contemporary technology.) This is serious and makes people miserable, and even leads to suicide, especially where bullying has taken place. Having a strategy to understand perfectionism and counter it, therefore, is a vital part of anyone's well-being toolkit. Again, it doesn't mean not striving to be better, to look fitter or more attractive; these are parts of our intrinsic human needs and provide self-confidence and esteem. As with most things in life, a balance is needed, knowing when desired outcomes have tilted over into obsession.

In summary, it is not perfectionism that is the cause of the problem. It is the human frailties which made it necessary in the first place. It is as if the perfect house we keep trying to build and maintain has no foundations to support it, hence the extraordinary and exhausting efforts which are required to keep the house from crumbling down.

# The perfectionism questionnaire

I have devised a few questions to help you decide if you might be edging towards unhelpful perfectionism. If you feel it doesn't apply to you, then either move on, or read through for interest. If you do score highly, then don't take it as a personal sleight, or even the hint of any kind of disorder. I am merely giving you some sort of analytical diagnostic so that you can self-assess your own leanings towards perfectionism or otherwise. Use it as a stimulant for reflection and read the tips on pages 112–114 to see what action you can take to correct.

## Self-Reflection: Are you a perfectionist?

It's a good idea to aim for excellence, but it is easy to push it too far. Not everything needs to be perfect, and if we strive for that and don't achieve it, we can fall into an *unhelpful perfectionism* spiral as we saw on pages 104–105. This kind of behaviour can paralyse you, and cause stress. Aim to be prudently perfect—that is, choose your battles, and be aware if the fear of not being perfect causes you to shrink back and avoid challenges. It is better to try and fail than not to try at all, wouldn't you agree?

The series of questions below are simply designed to challenge you and determine if you might fall into unhelpful perfectionism, and then for you to see where you might need to be more aware. It is interesting, as some people who see themselves as perfectionists can score low on this questionnaire. What it really gets at is not to ascertain whether you are committed to high standards, or conversely, you are a bit slapdash with everything, but more if your behaviour is driven by fear of failure. If it is the latter, this is worthy of personal reflection. As I have said, I don't think there is anything wrong with wanting everything to be the best it can be, but that's the point. The best it can be—not the best that's out of reach without unreasonable effort.

So, complete the following questionnaire if you are curious in this area. As with all such studies, try not to overthink this. You have two options, yes or no. There are no maybes. Just go with your first instinct, then move on. Each yes or no has a score. And of course, they are cunningly disguised so that you shouldn't really be saying, 'Okay I have got enough "Yes's" now. I need to put in a few "No's" to make me look more balanced.' I have mixed them up a bit. It shouldn't take more than five to six minutes to complete. And it goes without saying, don't try to be perfect at this!

## Perfectionism Questionnaire

| Question | Circle if 'Yes' | Circle if 'No' |
|---|---|---|
| Do you think people avoid working with you because of your impossibly high standards? | 2 | 1 |
| Do you complete a task to meet your own standards, even if someone else's expectations of you are higher? | 1 | 2 |
| Are you afraid of making mistakes because it will make you look bad to others? | 2 | 1 |

| Question | Circle if 'Yes' | Circle if 'No' |
|---|---|---|
| Do you tend to avoid taking on a task or hobby unless you can be perfect/amazing/brilliant at it? | 2 | 1 |
| Do you find it easy to get started on a project without worrying about a perfect outcome? | 1 | 2 |
| If you plan to entertain guests at home, do you get put off doing it if it can't be perfect? | 2 | 1 |
| Are you upset if you experience setbacks in a project, even if the result will still get you 'over the line'? | 2 | 1 |
| Do you get something finished first, then refine it? | 1 | 2 |
| Do you concern yourself more about the small details in a task rather than the overall result? | 2 | 1 |
| Do you find it easy to know when a task is done? | 1 | 2 |
| Do you criticise yourself if your result falls short of your ideal? | 2 | 1 |
| Do you spend a disproportionately long time on the last 10% of something to finish it perfectly? | 2 | 1 |
| Do you find it difficult to make decisions because there are no perfect solutions? | 2 | 1 |
| Do you enjoy receiving feedback so that you can improve on your work? | 1 | 2 |
| Do you frequently seek reassurance that your work is of a sufficiently high standard? | 2 | 1 |
| Are you confident about speaking up in conversation even if you say the wrong thing? | 1 | 2 |
| If you don't perform a daily ritual which will improve your day, do you worry that you will have a bad one? | 2 | 1 |
| Total Score | | |

If you have a score of >23 then review the questions and see where it most applied to you. i.e. look at the '2' scores. Do these indicate that you are heading towards unhealthy or unhelpful perfectionism. Let's review some actions you could take to balance the need for excellence with going over the top and trying to be perfect.

Firstly, think about what you do well. It's good to start here as we are more likely to stay positive if we start that way. Answer the questions below in your notebook:

- What is good about your perfectionist tendencies?
- Do you pick and choose where you need to be perfect (i.e., in work rather than home life)?
- Where has this helped you, and how?
- Where might it have caused problems?

If you are a high scorer in the questionnaire i.e., over 23, here are some guidance actions you might take:

1. **Have the courage to fail.** Review a time where you refused to take on an activity because you wanted to be perfect at it? What drove that perfection? Did you want to be the best? Was it pride? Were you afraid of failure or ridicule? Would you do anything differently now?

2. When reviewing an activity you did, and felt that your standards weren't met, can you reframe the outcome and **list down what you achieved**, not what you didn't? For example, a few weeks ago

I made a small wooden table for the garden. No really, I did! – I had to glue together the lengthways pieces and leave them overnight, clamped, so they would set. One of the pieces is out of whack and sticks out a small bit from the rest of the table. The perfectionist in me looks at the bit that sticks out and it almost seems like a failure. If I look at what I achieved, I did the following.

a) Designed a table to be self-made by an amateur carpenter (me).

b) Measured up and got the pieces cut at the DIY store.

c) Came up with a plan of work and an approach to get it finished.

d) Set aside time from my work schedule to fit in the build and still look after my business.

e) Put together at least 90% of the constituent parts almost 'perfectly'.

f) Problem solved and approached the task into bitesize chunks.

g) Everything was done in the right order and no re-work was necessary.

h) Stained the table and it is now fit for purpose, and if I say so myself looks reasonably attractive!

Look at all the things I did at least quite well. My eye is drawn to the piece that sticks out, and I am only talking about 3 mm. You can barely see it. I was afraid of my friends seeing it and making fun of my skills. Now, having reviewed this list, I feel I can stick my chest out and say I had a go!

Think of your own example of something you did but was not perfect. List the parts of the task you did well. List some things where you might do it differently next time.

Sometimes tasks can be daunting when you think about the final, finished, perfect product. **Break tasks down into small chunks as above.** It doesn't seem so daunting then and will organise you to do something better than you might have without decent planning probably.

3. **Consider why you won't start something**
   a) Is it because you are afraid of looking stupid if it goes wrong?
   b) Are you afraid of saying/doing the wrong thing?
   c) Are you worrying about factors outside of your control?
   d) Are you worried that you will give yourself a hard time if you fail?
   e) Are you avoiding doing something because you are afraid of feeling a failure or self-critical?

Write down some thoughts in your notebook if you want to. Committing your fears to paper (i.e., 'I am scared of looking stupid in presentations'), can help you diminish the fear and realise it's overblown when you look at simple words on a page.

Remember I talked about my philosophy that 90% is good enough? If you are a 100% perfectionist, then you might be worried that you must be perfect at removing your perfectionism! Don't throw the baby out with the bathwater. 90% of what you do is already very good—you just need to dial back rather than change yourself completely. This is why I call this Prudent Perfectionism. Pick your battles and keep what works for you. The most important point is to keep asking why? Why do I not do that? Why am I afraid of making a mistake in front of those people? Maybe those people don't really matter, or if they do, challenge your perspective about how they will react to you making a mistake or not seeming to be good enough. If you make a presentation to your team, they are not expecting perfection. They are not judging you as much as you think they are. Most people are more worried about themselves. They may make snap judgements on you which are not sufficiently evidence based. But you can't do a thing about that. So why kill yourself to try—to be good is good enough. Aim for that.

Now make some solid commitments to yourself on areas you might change here. These should be action based—you are going to DO something differently, and in this area, it usually involves trying something new, daring to go against your safety instincts and being brave. Use this simple template below to make your commitment. Be specific!

## Prudent Perfectionism commitments!

Perfectionism is a tough habit to break. You need to make some solid commitments to yourself so that you have something to measure yourself by. Follow these prompts below in your notebook, and make sure you can reference them easily!

- What I would like to improve on (e.g. overcoming fear of mistakes, accepting 90% etc.)
- Specific Action
- Where I will do it
- When
- Whose help do I need?

## Ignition Stage Remedies/Tool 3/ The Wheel of Life

**The Wheel of Life** will let you step back and assess at this stage how much focus you place on each part of your life and where you need to be in the foreseeable future. If, for example, you are going to be working harder, then you might have to accept, in the interests of keeping your marriage, that your hobbies take a back seat.

You can't be all things to all people. You can't do everything all at once and keep all those plates spinning. How often have you tried though, and feel that you probably have to because if you don't—who will? I know there are times when you have to hold down a demanding job, feed kids, do the laundry, keep an eye on an ageing parent, find time for a coffee with a friend in need. Sometimes you just have to grit your teeth through all that, as such circumstances are usually fleeting, and if they are not, then you need to take a look at where you can save time.

When our current calendars and schedules run out at the end of the year, we look at January and seem to have lots of space to do things. So, we start to fill up our time slots with stuff which will keep us busy, then we realise that our current commitments are still there and catch up with us.

We often delude ourselves that two or three months hence, which looks quiet in our calendars now, will be any less busy than our current schedule. Counting back the same amount of time into the past, we thought we weren't going to be busy now, but we are, aren't we? It is an illusion therefore, that, we will be quieter in a few months' time, and we will have more time to spare than right now. People say it all the time. Let me get this project out of the way, then we can focus on that. Take as much care about what you schedule to do farther in the future, as you would next week. If you don't plan choicefully, your time will drift away from you. We will see this start to bite on Rung 3: Neglect, as we sacrifice activities because of time absorbed by work.

The Wheel of Life will help you look at how much attention you place on certain aspects of your life and give you more choice about what you want to spend your time on in the next quarter. You can then use other planning tools which work for you to make sure it happens!

Don't spend too much time filling this in. It's not an exact science, more a feeling. As you start the exercise with scoring where you are now, make sure you reflect on the last few months, not just today, in case you have a weird week when you are on holiday or something. Think big picture and trends, not isolated events. For example, if you wanted to score much higher on cultivating friendships, and you had one coffee with a friend you haven't seen in years, but that is about it, then that can't really score very high. It is easy to get a halo glow from doing one thing and thinking you have fixed it but take the action in context with everything else.

## Exercise: Draw your Wheel

The headings are left blank for you to choose your own, but here are a few ideas in case you are not sure: Work, Hobbies, Family, House (i.e., DIY), Relationship, Friends, Social, Personal, Growth, Health, Fun, etc.

You can place a mark for how low or high your emphasis is on this current area of your life—the closer to the centre of the circle is low and further out is high. The marks go on the lines related to each heading.

1. Join the marks so you get a sense of the shape.

2. Look and see what the general shape is. How balanced is it? Are there any areas you are neglecting?

3. Now you could take a different colour and mark where you would like it to be, or where a change

might take you in the next time period (quarter/half-year/year).

4. See from this where you might need to make a shift in prioritisation. If you would like to make any changes and increase your focus in one area—will another have to give?

5. There are no rights or wrongs here—it is up to you how you balance your life (but a general rule might be that if your focus is high in a lot of areas—you could be burning out).

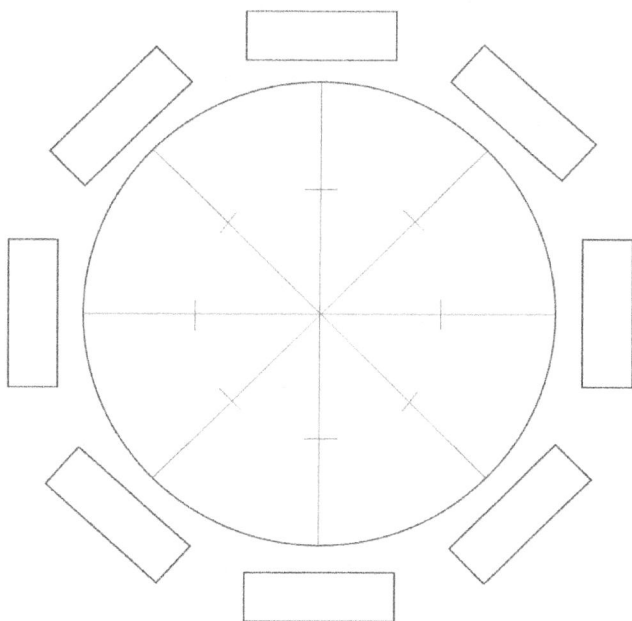

## Notes / Actions

---

---

## Stop worrying that you *can't* do it

The Ignition stage is a pivot point for change. Decisions are made here, and action is imminent. I am concerned that I might be frightening you too much by encouraging you to think of all the reasons why you shouldn't be taking on a new responsibility. We are, I believe, far more capable of doing good work and achievement than we think we might be because our inner critic (the negative voice in our head which judges us) holds us back. Often, we allow the fear to mask the fact that, at the top, there could be a magnificent view. I am going to cover this more in the next rung of the ladder, ACCELERATION, because outright self-criticism is as bad as blind arrogance. We should know that our limits are probably higher than we think they are, but there usually *are* limits. It's not fair to expect everyone to be able to be the CEO of a major multi-national, or to be an accomplished electrician. Human achievement has largely been arrived at by looking at the limits of our current capability and then pushing those boundaries just that little bit further. Look at American-manned space flight in the 1960s. The Soviet Union was crushing the US in the early stages of the space race, always one step ahead in the next milestone. The key turning point other than, as it turned out, having the most resources, was John F. Kennedy's publicly stated goal: 'Before this decade is out, [we will] land a man on the moon, and return him safely to the Earth.' The goal galvanised the American effort, but each step had to be meticulously planned out, achievements built on the ones before. When he first made this bold assertion, NASA had not even flown an astronaut successfully on a complete orbit of our planet. They learned how to reliably launch rockets without them blowing up, then navigate in space, communicate with Earth, dock spacecraft, come back down safely, then, finally, traverse the void to the moon and land softly upon it. Incremental steps all the way. It is an astonishing human achievement that this happened with the technology available at the time, but they did it. Scarcely anyone who was not just blindly patriotic really was convinced they would meet the president's goal. We can and do make more of ourselves than we think we are capable of.

# CHAPTER 7
# RUNG 2: ACCELERATION

Changes are afoot, and not only afoot, but in progress. Your foot has hit the gas pedal, and you feel the exhilarating push back into the seat as you thrust forward. It feels like a thrill as your adrenaline surges, and you start to get up for the battles ahead.

This is undoubtedly the most seductive step up The Burnout Ladder®. You are beckoned in, and the mind and body, with its resources to enable you to harness energy and make things happen, click into overdrive. Adrenaline gives you the necessary boost to get going and keep going. Dopamine motivates you to repeat more of whatever it is that's rewarding you. Endorphins give you pleasure as you go through pain. You are working more because you might be enjoying the work itself, or just the idea of working harder is giving you a self-boost. You get a buzz as others start to notice your efforts and that you are clearly putting in some extra work—that one is ultra-dangerous for the people-pleasers (i.e., most of us), as the reward for getting noticed is to want to do more of it.

My experience in burnout was to fill my body with stress hormones and push through, and the rewards came from the recognition I would receive that I was doing my bit and more, but also my own sense of self-righteousness that I was working very hard and that was surely the right thing to do. I know now that I was fulfilling some need to prove something to myself, a gap in my previous experience which made me feel as if I had fallen short somewhere and needed to pay it back. This is clearly some kind of Impostor Syndrome variant; the feeling that I haven't earned the right to be here, and one day, I would surely be found out. At this stage of the ladder, the price of hard work seems worth it, because the reward of feel-good outweighs the pain of extra effort. You may be in top gear too and enjoying the flow state we talked about in Chapter 6: Rung 1: Ignition. The work is consuming you, but in a good way because you are enjoying it. Forcing yourself to be more efficient so that you can get through everything, you are prioritising well, only focusing on stuff that matters and not tinkering around the edges. This means that you will be creative too, finding ways to cover ground and solve problems that you didn't think were possible. You are energised, as you are in peak condition to face the challenge, and your mind and body are up to it.

You become attached to these little tonics and boosts you get from putting the extra yards in, but like any addict, you must keep upping the dose to get the same rewards. There is a double impact as this grips you.

You need to do more of this to get the same payback, so you start to fatigue, and then you begin to neglect your other commitments as you work later into the night and log in at weekends. At this stage, there is enjoyment and comfort in that. It will all be okay if you just keep trying, even as you begin to drown under your larger workload, so you must be doing the right thing here. Then, of course, as people see you doing more, you become a work magnet. To paraphrase an adage, 'If you want something to do well, give it to someone who is busy.' There's more than an ounce of truth in that. When you're busy, you get into flow state. You don't overthink, you just get on with it and cut out the irrelevancies. Another reason why you get pulled onto the Burnout Ladder®, because you feel good about being the go-to employee. Of course, you do; this will enrich your chances of survival through the crisis. Crisis? Yes, it's certainly coming, even if you can't see it yet.

## Not all is rosy in the garden

This rung of the ladder is full of promise and feel-good factors, as I have outlined above. But sadly, a few dark clouds have appeared on the horizon too. When you set out on this journey, you will have had some expectations of yourself that you were entirely up to the task, but there may be elements where you feel now that you lack the guns. This is quite normal if you are asked to step up a level in your organisation. There may be a logical reason why you were at the level you were at and you might not have been quite ready for the jump. In my case, I made a leap but didn't have formal authority. I was given a temporary title, Acting Director, which is not the same as Director. Naturally, with this title, you might feel inferior to someone who is talented enough already to do the job proper. Of course, this may have been to some extent true, but on the other hand, would my boss have asked me to step up if he didn't think I could do it? Who knows what the truth of that is, but it's worth stopping and considering that there were two realities there. One was that I was going into that situation with some (but not all) the skills and experience that I needed. The other was that I let the 'Acting' label hold me down like a weight attached to my ankle.

So, where are we then on this ladder? What is happening to you and what do you need to do to prevent you from climbing it further? We have talked about the excitement of new work and responsibility. The brain loves novelty after all, as well as challenge. There are thrills at being noticed for your hard work and the knowledge that people are thinking well of you. You bet they are if you have conveniently solved a problem for them.

But at this time in your ascent, you will find that a few cracks start to show. It may not be your fault, but how you react to it will be entirely up to you. It's so easy to allow negative thoughts and feelings to creep in after an initial burst of confidence. It is probable that you are riding high in this stage of the ladder, giving you a touch of swagger. You might just have been promoted or given extra responsibility because of the merit of your performance. This can lead to an initial feeling that you can conquer the world. You may forget that you are stepping up, and thoughts of challenges recede as you feel invincible. There is a pulse of enthusiasm and over-optimism. That's a feature of this stage. Soon enough though, reality can bite. Someone doesn't agree with the process you wanted to implement; a team member doesn't have time to take on the extra work you need them to do. A manager in another department thinks you are stepping out of your lane with a new initiative. The world can often look much easier while planning something on your laptop or in your mind than when it comes time to implement. Real people and situations often make life very difficult!

When gaps start to show in what you can deliver, then certain negative thoughts will start to dominate. There are elements of frustration about the circumstances you are in and the lack of commitment, perhaps, of people around you. Perhaps they are not quite so invested in this as you. You might have expected more support. Yet, after a while, the finger of blame which you pointed outwards often turns inwards on you. This happens because when the wheels start to wobble, most of us will eventually question our own ability to make things happen. If someone has a bad attitude on our team, then it must be at least partly our fault for not being able to motivate them. I personally think this is not always a bad thing. It is all too easy to blame others when events don't go well. If we have nothing to fix in ourselves, then how can we shape anything to get better? If it's not us, then who is it? Our 'inner critic' is a useful aide, but also a towering bully. If its voice is too loud, it will distort our thinking and beliefs and stop us from reaching our potential. It will prevent us from trying new ideas and projects because it will think we will fail. It is trying to protect us, but it ultimately harms us. And at this stage of the ladder, it will skew us off into unnecessary doubts, consume our energy, and possibly assist in making us fail. How can this happen? How can we start out so positively and then allow ourselves to dive mentally?

Allow me to paint a picture about how we can start veering in this negative direction.

## Faulty models lead to faulty thinking

In Chapter 2: Causes of Burnout, we discussed the mental models we create to navigate the world. (If you have skipped to this chapter, I strongly recommend you go back to that and have a read through that section, although I will provide a short summary for you here. See! People-pleaser…) In summary, we build mental maps, or models, of our environment to help us understand it, navigate our way through it, and to predict what we might need to anticipate. These models are built from experiences and memories, often distorted versions of realities because of a negative twist we apply in stressful situations. These models form our beliefs and perceptions to how we see the world.

This view we have created subconsciously via our modelling, then becomes the driving factor behind conscious thoughts. It has been said, but what we think, we very often become. Our ability to think is the secret of our success as a species, but it is a double-edged sword. We have the ability not only to dream up solutions to problems and invent wheels and light bulbs, but also the mind can allow its survival bias to imagine disastrous situations which require our mental energy to avert, even if the outcome was highly unlikely. *The beliefs we have from the inaccurate models that we build, programme us to think and act consistent with that world view.*

We sometimes feel shackled to our thoughts. And no wonder. They get stuck in our heads and go round and round like a disc on a turntable. Our thinking is done via our *neurons*, of which we have around 86 billion. Neurons are communication cells within the brain and body which pass on messages to each other via an electrical charge. These charges travel across tiny gaps between adjacent neuron cells called *synapses*. The complexity and sophistication of this methodology is astounding, and I am going to drastically oversimplify for both our sakes. Neural pathways are highly complex, and involve trillions of connections, but when we form an established pathway for the signals to pass, then the more we do it, the more accomplished that pathway becomes. As the phrase goes, 'Neurons that fire together, wire together.' The more we establish a path, the better we can do something. The better we get, then the more the neural pathway becomes grooved, and so becomes habitual. For example, if we learn to play a musical instrument, the neurons associated with that activity fire and wire together the more we do it.

If we wanted to speak a foreign language but don't practice, the neurons and synaptic connections do not develop in the same way. Our thinking as well as our doing, is governed by these linkages. The more we think negatively, the better we get at it. It becomes an entrenched habit.

## Neuroplasticity

We have an incredible ability to adapt our neural pathways. Those synapses across which signals are passed are gaps, not solid matter. This gives us more ability to 'rewire' across different synapses if our brain chooses, because those connections are not 'hard-wired'. When we are born, we have all the neural networks we are going to need, but the connections are not yet established. Over time, we pare back the connections we use, as the energy required to maintain the whole potential network would be exhausting. Synaptic pruning is where we effectively mothball certain connections while we focus on others. It's like a map of the country where all the towns and cities have been built, and the space for the roads have been allocated but they have not yet been built. Over time, some become established, and some are just left as wild land, but always having the potential to be developed. What this means is that we have the capability of developing new neural networks and connections if we want to, so we are more adaptable in taking on new skills. This also applies to thinking too, of course. We might get tired of the same old thoughts whizzing round our heads, but we are not stuck with them. We can build new networks, new ways of thinking and acting. This is called *neuroplasticity*, because like Plasticine, the modelling clay I remember from my childhood, our brains can be moulded.

## Like the models that lead to them, thoughts are not real

Negative thoughts can dominate us, ruining our mood and our general state of mental health. The problem has become so widespread that Cognitive Behavioural Therapy (CBT) has become a go-to remedy prescribed by a lot of doctors for anxiety and depression. I am a big supporter as I have been through it myself, and it is better than taking drugs. However, it's not the be-all and end-all. CBT is mainly about correcting patterns of conscious thinking and consequently changing behaviours. It's a talking therapy which gets quicker results than years of psychoanalysis. While this seems attractive, the caveat is that our thinking is not just from the brain. It is a result of emotion, feelings, deep down experiences, and even trauma. CBT is a logical solution to what are often emotional problems. That said, a thought can influence a feeling as much as the other way round, so if we can train ourselves to think better, or more accurately and usually positively, then we will naturally feel better.

Brain and body work in feedback loops. Messages are passed and action is taken if necessary. The brain monitors the situation in the body at any given time, so it is aware of any problems which arise. Later, when I talk in more depth about emotions (Chapter 9: Rung 4: Cynicism), I also discuss the feelings which drive those emotions. A feeling can and does shape a thought. If we have a feeling that someone has just been rude to us, we are more likely to be negative in your thinking about a situation as opposed to hearing nice compliments. It works both ways too. If you can train your brain to have more positive thoughts, then the feelings and emotions which are present can also shift. It is just more difficult the other way, since it is harder to change the way we feel than it is to change the way you think. Feelings are visceral, primal and emotionally charged. They are difficult to change, but we can train ourselves to respond in the way we think *about* them. Let's say that the words a person used about us seemed to come across negatively, and this feeling of hurt or betrayal or whatever it was impacted our thinking. A thought may arise from feelings and emotions such as 'harsh!' or 'that's not fair' or 'they hate me.' You could, if you trained yourself, come up with some alternative thinking as follows:

Harsh > Direct
That's not fair > Let's examine all the facts before deciding that
They hate me > One comment does not necessarily denote hatred

One other issue with CBT is that it is effective when in a rational state of mind. If we feel as if our integrity or character is under attack from someone, then the amygdala will trigger the fight-or-flight alarm, and so we might end up fighting fire with fire, rather than taking the higher ground. Balanced thinking is difficult under pressure. It is something which comes with practice but might also be a tactic which you use when not in a live situation but on the training ground, so to speak. In other words, don't beat yourself up for reacting emotionally in the moment, but if you can learn to think more constructively in all the hours of soul-searching that you do, then this can make a huge difference to your mental health.

Often, we are guilty of 'faulty thinking' and since this governs much of our lives—we are never far from our thoughts, after all—it is as well to do some work here. Our thoughts can shape our day, as we find it almost impossible to not think any. Neuroscientists have found that when our minds are at rest, that is, not focusing on solving or achieving something, we have the tendency to utilise regions of the brain called the *default mode network*, which, amongst other things, leaves us brooding on the intentions of others. Since we are so dependent on connection and it is a fundamental drive for us, this is something which hurts if we get it wrong. Isolation from others leaves us to gap-fill others' thoughts and intentions which are often inaccurate in our model, as we have discussed already. This is one category of thinking which will be discussed in the table below, as well as how we relate to others.

Let's just home in a bit more on thoughts. What even is a thought, now we come to think of it? They are, of course, a product of all that neural activity and general going-ons with our feelings and emotions. I will list some points about them to keep front of mind:

## Thoughts on thoughts

1. Thoughts become habits if unchecked—just the same as physical ones, such as smoking.

2. Thoughts are not real—they are mental events. Like any of our neural pathways, they are not hardwired and so we are not, or should not be, defined by our thoughts. They can be changed and replaced with new events.

3. It is easy to be hard on ourselves for thinking something bad—even if we should not—but it helps if we then acknowledge the thoughts we are having with acceptance and look for alternatives if thinking patterns are weighing us down.

4. A negative bias is inevitable as an evolved attribute—which makes us, on average, more negative than positive. If we are aware of this, then it can help us to know that it's an operating system design fault. We can tweak the software in our brains, however, moving more towards the positive.

5. Thoughts are influenced by feeling and emotion; it is so difficult to change feelings when

they happen so quickly. Feelings have been programmed into us since before we developed brains, so it is impractical to want to override that. It is hard to change the way we feel, but we can change the way we think about how we feel.

What I have found helpful personally, and with coaching others, is to recognise patterns of thinking. Once we call them out and label them, then the thoughts, in a sense, know they are being monitored and that they are now exposed and vulnerable to scrutiny. It helps to have awareness of what we are actually thinking and being able to break the patterns. Once we have done this, then we can steer our thinking down a new neural path. We can build new roads and let the old, unhelpful ones decay. Beware, though, that we need to keep a vigil. There may be deeper emotional reasons for experiencing the thoughts that we do, and so often, if those basics are not addressed, the thoughts come back. Sometimes, too, we need to let thoughts out, as it were. Just pushing them away and denying them means they will come back even stronger. Acknowledge, accept, then change direction.

## Faulty thinking categories

These categories of thinking have been derived from a number of sources, and I have chosen the ones I find most useful, as well as simplifying them to make this into a practical tool.

Our brains predict the future as a survival need so as much as we like to stay in the present, we don't like surprises. Hence, the need for building those mental models I have described. We try and tell what the future will be by piecing together bits of information from data we do NOT have. Predicting the future so we can be ready for it is called **Fortune-telling**. It leads us to second guess and make some inaccurate assumptions about where we are headed. Nobody knows what the future holds, even if we think we can predict somebody's behaviour. If we find ourselves predicting something, then we might fulfil the prophecy by making it happen anyway. If we go into a meeting with a predisposed view on what someone else is going to say, then guess what? We might have a part to play in making them behave like that.

When we are predicting how someone is going to behave or what they are going to say, or even what they might be thinking this very moment, that is known as **Mind Reading**. Of course, it is another calculation designed to enable us to react to the intentions of others, which could be quite useful, of course. We may have actually upset someone, and we might try to calculate how we can make it up to them. But there is a tendency to get stuck in this mode, and the thinking becomes the norm rather than exception. Going round and round in circles and overthinking, we get away from anything grounded in fact or might serve any practical purpose. It just becomes rumination.

When we worry about the future and how it might play out, we can get caught in **Catastrophising**.

Another magnificent survival feature, this is where we use our imagination to play out the worst possible scenarios that could happen to us in the event of something going off plan. I used to be embarrassed about relating this cruel fear, but I now know that I am not alone. If I wasn't doing well at work, or it looked like a project was going to fail and I was at least partly culpable, then the following sequence of events played themselves out in my head: a) poor year-end review, b) I would be identified as a prime target for removal from the business, c) lose job, d) can't get another job, e) lose house, f) lose marriage, g) homeless, and h) I'm living under a bridge.

I don't want to in any way make light of this, as this sadly is the plight of some unfortunate people. My point is that the probability of this happening to me in those times was very low, and in fact, hasn't happened yet, so in hindsight, the chances were zero. Of course, a) and b) could have happened. Percentages of low performing employees are routinely targeted by large companies for being 'managed out' each year in an evolutionary process to improve standards of work and cut costs. I am sure that if I had indeed lost my job I could have got another one. You could argue that it is this fear which keeps us sharp, but there is a middle ground between complacency and terror.

When we catastrophise, we imagine extreme outcomes to routine problems. Research has shown that we are overly pessimistic at forecasting pessimistic outcomes, and so we should take care to bear this in mind. Most events don't end up so bad as we thought, and we should check ourselves when predicting a future which has no base in evidence from past experience.

Another technique to counter this that I have heard others use is called *catastrophic thinking reversal.* This is where you can use humour to have some fun with your ruinous prophecies. In this case, you do think of your worst-case scenario and then exaggerate it. If you were worried about an important presentation at work, you could indulge your worst fear that you will forget everything you were going to say and that everyone will laugh at you. Then, the windows shatter and your trousers fall down, leaving you standing, giggling in your pants. As you open your mouth to speak, the words come out of your mouth like Donald Duck. Everyone collapses in fits of laughter. While this may seem extreme, that is exactly the point, and it will give your brain a jolt and allow you to poke fun at yourself, releasing some tension. There are few things better than humour to diffuse stress and get your brain thinking straight again.

On a similar vein, but with a twist, we can also bend reality in terms of past happenings and think ourselves into a stew by **Overgeneralising**. Catch yourself saying, 'They always do that,' and this is one way of overgeneralisation. 'Always' means they do that every time, not just once or twice. If someone has done something that you don't like, and only once or twice, the memory can pick up on this and build it into its model. So, this is why they *always* do it.

Another form of overgeneralising is **Extrapolation**. Isn't it funny how one bad thing happens, and everything is ruined? One meeting didn't go well, so it's probably the death knell for the project. These are natural anxieties which creep in as self-doubts take over, and the imagination allows us to think of the bad stuff rather than the good. We can take one unfortunate minor incident and use that to define our day.

Which is a lovely segue into **All-or-Nothing Thinking**. In some ways, this is the specialist domain of the perfectionist. I won't have that party unless it's perfect. If I don't look my absolute best, then I am not going out tonight. It means we don't do something unless it can be just right. I know there is a mindset which says, 'If a job is worth doing, it's worth doing right.' But right doesn't have to mean perfect or everything. Another phrase I like is, 'Don't let perfect be the enemy of good.' As I said in the Perfectionism section in Chapter 6: Rung 1: Ignition, the mindset of 'this will be average or good' will help you get off the starting blocks. Not everything in life is black and white. We get put off doing good things by these polarised views of the world.

**Mental Filtering**. Have you ever spoken in public or made a presentation and the meeting went swimmingly, and you have been lavished with praise for the good job you have done, except for the one thing that you said that you could have done differently. Isn't this the thing you dwell on when you're driving home? It's that old chestnut, survival, once again. 'Don't be complacent, don't be arrogant,' says the voice on your shoulder. If you do, then something is bound to sneak up and get you! So, you keep scanning around for what you are not good at and when someone calls you out on it, then you say to yourself, 'Ah, ha, I knew it!' and so it reinforces the model.

If you think the world is all about you, then you would be wrong. We each live in our bubble which to us, of course, seems very large and encompassing other people's bubbles. This is **Egocentric Thinking**. Many things others do or say seem like a personal sleight to you. Either their values are different and so you judge them, or you think that their actions may even be a deliberate sleight to you. Their minds are full of stuff happening to them, not you. If your friend seems sulky when you first meet up, your natural negative bias might think that it is something you have done or said, but it's almost certain that it isn't. We are all prey to feelings within us that drive our emotions, and they can be due to hunger or if it's raining and cold. Our moods are generally dictated from within, not from outside. It's not all about you!

**Emotional Reasoning**. Every thought or action we ever make goes through a filter of emotions and predictions based on our experiences, many of them emotional. We should indeed listen to our guts, be aware of feeling, and certainly not ignore it. So, this is not what I am talking about.

Emotional reasoning is when feelings become facts. For example, I feel ill, therefore I ate something bad last night. Or, I feel tired, so I am going to flunk my job interview today. Feelings are only a part of the picture; they are not the whole truth of the situation at all. We need the facts as well to redress the balance.

This kind of thinking sets us off on the wrong path. The job interview prediction was one based on fear of failure, not fact or any other experience we may have had. When you catch yourself using feelings to predict an outcome, see if you can identify whether there is any factual substance to it.

If you feel that your inner critic is pointing the finger at you, then you might like to think of this final faulty thinking category. It is not so much inaccurate thoughts; it is more the demanding nature of our brains on ourselves. Look out for the words '**Must**' or '**Should**.'

> 'I *must* get my act together.'
> 'I *should* really be better at that.'

These kinds of directions, which are self-directed thoughts in essence, can cause us to put too much pressure on ourselves and cause us to tighten up our mental muscles, leading to a fight-or-flight, on the back foot kind of response rather than a contented, creative one. They are thinking errors because, really, who says you *must* or *should* do anything? These are the kinds of mental bullies living within us, which we frankly need to hear less from.

## Acceleration Stage Remedies/Tool 4/ Faulty Thinking

It might take some time to learn all of these categories, and you don't need to do so by heart. The way to use this tool is to refer to it when you start to recognise habitual thoughts that you have. There are some that we repeat over and over. Start with those, then checking which category they fall into, you can start to label them to yourself next time you become aware that they crop up in your head. Ways to correct, new ways of thinking, are suggested in the right-hand column of the diagram.

| Thought Bias | Examples of Faulty Thinking | Ways to Correct |
| --- | --- | --- |
| Fortune-telling | • I know that's going to happen<br>•This is going to be awful | • You can't predict the future<br>• Think instead: what is the worst that can happen?<br>• That whatever happens, I will deal with it; I trust myself |
| Mind Reading (others' thoughts and actions) | • They won't like this<br>• I can tell they don't want me | • Never assume; ask<br>• I will leave my mind open to the reaction I get |
| Catastrophising | • If that goes wrong, it's all over<br>• If I don't hit my sales target, I could lose my job, my home, and my family | • Think of the worst-case scenario but also the best case so you get some balance<br>• Try catastrophic thinking reversal to have some fun with the situation |

| Thought Bias | Examples of Faulty Thinking | Ways to Correct |
|---|---|---|
| Overgeneralisation | • I failed at that project; my reputation is in tatters!<br>• They always do that! | • Weigh up the evidence<br>• Has everything gone wrong—really? Think of the positives you learned<br>• Do they really ALWAYS do that? Think further—what other behaviours do they show? |
| Extrapolation | • They weren't together at the party; therefore, they must be splitting up<br>• I got a negative comment on my post; it's not hitting the right notes | • Get your rounded facts and data before jumping to conclusions<br>• Watch out for Mental Filtering (below) |
| All-or-Nothing Thinking | • I won't host Christmas unless it can be perfect<br>• If I can't lay guitar like Mark Knopfler, then I won't bother | • Remember that nothing is perfect<br>• Better to be decent or good than not to try<br>• Think instead: I will do the best I can do in the circumstances |
| Mental Filtering | • I knew they would pick up on that thing I said<br>• (After hearing six things they said were good about your presentation): It failed because I didn't hammer home that point | • Think of your mind as a prosecution attorney<br>• It presents the evidence in a biased manner<br>• At any moment, your defence lawyer will stand up and assert your innocence |

| Thought Bias | Examples of Faulty Thinking | Ways to Correct |
|---|---|---|
| Must's and Should's | • I should know that<br>• I must nail that presentation | • Reset your expectations; are you setting yourself up?<br>• Constantly question your 'must' and 'should' statements |
| All-or-Nothing | • It must be 100% perfect<br>• I need to look perfect or I am not going out | • Think of progress made, not the gap (does anyone get 100% in an exam?)<br>• What is 'good enough?' Recalibrate |
| Egocentric Thinking | • I would never be late like that; they obviously don't care about me | • Understand that your values are different to others<br>• It is not a personal sleight against you |
| Emotional Reasoning | • I feel useless; therefore, I am not good enough | • Don't let emotions decide the decision<br>• What are the facts? |

*Figure 5. Faulty Thinking and how to correct it*

If you can capture the thinking and then re-examine it, you will see that there is almost always another view. Mental habits and established neural firing means that it is easier to keep thinking along the same lines. If we don't find ways to think better, then it will drag us down and sap our energy.

## Thoughts are not facts

We have already discussed this, but people do get bogged down here. When I teach this principle, people sometimes get a bit uppity. And yes, thoughts swirl around in our heads, are all-consuming and dictate our day and sometimes our lives. They certainly feel real. Some thoughts are real, for sure, but some are made up. Our thoughts mesh into each other and thoughts lead into one another in a stream or torrent. But if we can start to identify the thoughts by shining a light on them as we are learning to do here, we can distinguish between real and imaginary.

I recommend that you try labelling thoughts, as in the categorisation table above, as it will give you an easier way to see what is inside your head—in the same way that you would label pots of seed in a greenhouse, so you can know what is coming up through the soil and what to do with each type of plant.

Thought categorisation can be helpful to identify patterns, but it also provides a further understanding of what is real versus imaginary. By this, I mean there are some thoughts we have which are factual and practical. There is no other interpretation possible. There are others where the mind has already put a spin on them.

Let's look at a few typical thoughts which might cross our minds during the course of a day and examine them for what they are. There is no connection between these examples.

I am going to make a cup of tea now.
I am no good at gardening.
That motorbike noise was loud.
They might never speak to me again.

Some are factual, you could say. If you're going to make a cup of tea, and you are thinking about it, that's real. Equally, the motorbike was loud. They usually are. That's real—except you might want to think about your reaction to the motorbike sometimes. If you are trying to watch TV and the noise outside drowns out the sound, you will likely be annoyed, but it was a passing moment, and the irritation stays with us for longer. It is just a sound, and although you might focus on the selfishness of the rider, does that actually help you? Being aware of thoughts as they arise means they can be analysed and discarded, if necessary, then replaced with healthier thinking. The garden thought All-or-Nothing thinking, as there is surely a spectrum of ability here. The final one is Egocentric thinking, or even Mind Reading (doesn't matter which it is as long as you pick it out). The important point is to spot it and re-wire the neurons.

## Nourishers and Depleters

As we go through the weekly grind, we inevitably spend time doing things which we like and those which we don't. The balance tends to shift away from the ones you want to do, simply because most things we do are necessary and not that pleasant generally, or at least, they are boring and can drain us. Let's call these opposing types of activity **Nourishers** and **Depleters**. Most of the time, our Depleters are just something we have to do. Grocery shopping, cleaning, checking the weekly sales spreadsheet, filling out forms, paying bills, bank reconciliations. Classic examples of things that most of us don't like to do. On the other side of the coin, there are things which really drive us—going to the match, socialising, knitting, dancing, perhaps having 1-2-1 coffees with colleagues, or spending time alone with a book. These are the Nourishers and they are what we live for, giving us energy.

It's so easy to get caught up in the relentless doing and achieving mode of life, getting things done, ticking things off. There is an awful lot we do that is largely mundane. You might call them neutral experiences. Chores you don't mind doing, even though you hated the prospect of having to do them. They still deplete you if you approach them with the wrong mindset.

The simple strategy is to do more of the Nourishers. Don't forget, at times like these, what you love to do and what lights a fire in you. The Depleters, well, see what you could offload to someone else. If it is at work, there may be someone who loves the detail of reading through a contract that you were supposed to read, and they hate doing something that you like. Quid pro quo. It's a good exercise to do in a wider team. Set aside some time for a meeting (having first explained to those who hate meetings that, with any luck, they should leave feeling more nourished than depleted), and having asked everyone to prepare a list of their regular tasks or responsibilities, you can go through them all as a team and see what nourishes or depletes everybody (what an eye-opener this might be!), and then see if anything can be moved around in the group. The effort put in here for yourself and colleagues to avoid burnout cannot be underestimated. You could also do this at home. If you can nourish yourself more in your personal life, this will osmose into your work-self too.

It is natural to sacrifice the activities that we enjoy just to get on with the business of life, treading the hamster wheel just to keep surviving. As that happens, we start to live lives of monotony and dread, allowing energy to be depleted. This is not so important at this stage of the ladder, but it will really hit you later if you don't fix it now.

## Acceleration Stage Remedies/Tool 5/ Nourishers and Depleters

Here is a method for a) doing more of what nourishes you, b) doing less of what depletes you, and c) thinking differently about things you don't like so that they may even become a form of nourishment.

Think of a typical day or week. **Write down** any activities you do at least once in this time span. They are likely to be habitual repeating activities (i.e., emptying the dishwasher, going for a walk, cooking, playing guitar, school run, gardening, paying bills, commuting, meditating, exercising, playing cards, going to the pub, reading, sleeping, napping, laundry, ironing, cleaning, any *people* you spend time with?) **List** them down in your notebook. Just make sure you have covered activities which, when combined, take up the majority of your time. Now, with this list in mind, the words can be transferred into one of three categories below:

1. You love it and it Nourishes you.

2. You don't love it or hate it, but you do it anyway—you might consider your attitude to it neutral. May still dread the thought of doing it.

3. You hate it, or at least dislike it, and it Depletes your energy, especially the thought of doing it.

Make three columns in your notebook. Head them **I love this activity (Nourisher), Neither love nor hate (Neutral, mundane)**, and **Depleter (Hate it!)**.

Transfer the activities you wrote down into one of these three columns.

When you have completed transferring those activities into your table in your notebook, then put your pen down and look at it. How balanced does it look to you? Does there seem to be a bias towards any columns? It's not an exact 1:1 relationship, of course. Something which takes a lot of time may hardly nourish or deplete you at all, or one small thing may be derailing your day or bringing you joy.

Look, also, if anything is *missing*. When the chips are down, we tend to abandon those joyous activities which once lit us up. Equally, you may have ditched a burdensome activity or avoided seeing someone who drained you. In which case, give yourself a pat on the back for having made some steps in this area already!

Now it's action time. Make another table with two columns.

On the left-hand side (Nourishers), write down activities you are going to do more of—or start doing if you have let something slip. This could apply to people, of course. In the Chapter 10: Rung 5: Disengage, you will discover a neat way of figuring out who you need to see more of.

On the right-hand side (Depleters), be firm about activities you are going to do less of. And of course, this absolutely applies to people who are draining your energy somehow.

If you wrote anything down in the middle column, just leave this for the moment until we go onto the next stage.

So, what to do with all those things that you just apparently *have to do*. There is no shifting them. That's just life that you need to do the school run, drive to work, pay the bills, keep the house tidy. In almost all of these activities, the thought of doing them is worse than the doing themselves. There are a couple of methods here for making sure these don't deplete you but may actually become a form of nourishment.

## Reframing the mundane

Now, think of the items in the middle column. How might you think differently about them so that they don't become mindless Depleters. For example, you could use dish-washing time as a time to listen to a favourite podcast. Mowing the lawn could be a chance to stop and appreciate nature—a mindful moment. You can reframe anything that is a chore into a privilege, simply by changing '*I have to (do something)*' to '*I get to (do something)*.*' We take so many parts of our lives for granted. It is a miracle we are even here, and although we can't see it when we are stressed and under pressure, most of us lead privileged lives.

## Making the mindless mindful

Being mindful is appreciating the very moment you are in. Nothing else matters. And it can be a pleasure, not a chore, if only I allow my senses to overtake my thinking brain. Example. The bed linen has just been freshly laundered, and I have been asked to assist in ensuring it is fitted onto the bed. Deep groan as I drag myself away from Netflix. Oh noooo! I hate this. Such a dull activity, and I could be starting another episode of whatever it is I am binge-watching. That's my mind taking over. It seeks pleasure, and getting tangled up in duvet covers and vallances is not pleasurable. I am thinking about it, predicting that I will hate it, and so I hate it. What then, if a different approach is to stop thinking? What if I smell the fresh sheets and duvet cover as I take part in this activity? It is a very pleasant thing. I touch the sheets and move them between fingers and thumb to feel the cotton. Not a thought goes through my head, except perhaps to reframe the task as in the last paragraph and reflect that I will be lucky enough to sleep in clean sheets tonight when perhaps others may not be so fortunate.

## Commitments

Below you will find instructions for how you do more of what Nourishes you and less of what Depletes you. I ask you to add in to this a resolution to think differently about those middle column items, which possibly take up most of your day. They could make the most difference, if only you can introduce some gratitude and present-moment-enjoyment habits.

You can't do it all. Prioritise which actions you want to take and write a brief but precise action plan for how you will achieve it.

If you are going to use the 'force of habits' tool in this same section (read on), you will learn that the best way to make a new habit stick (or to lose one) is to be pinpoint-specific about when and where you are going to do something. Your brain doesn't like vague instructions. It will give you the run around and not do it.

**Make a list** of actions, and for each describe the action, where it'll happen, when it'll happen, and who it'll happen with (if necessary).

## The force of habits

In this tool, I am asking you to block out time for building or maintaining good habits in your daily routine, and the tool I offer gives you tips on how to do this. Why is this important? Well, you're still early in the ladder ascent. As things start to go well for you, you feel like you are riding this exciting train and that it is okay that some of your good habits go by the wayside. Equally, it is the time when bad habits start to creep in. As you start to wake earlier because your mind is consumed by all the things you must get done, you forget your meditation habit and your workout routine. You ensure you get a few cups of coffee to keep you going, to comfort you. I, myself, tend to cling onto little luxuries when I feel that life is all about work or responsibilities. While there is nothing wrong in savouring moments and having refuges, be careful that those activities don't end up depleting you rather than nourishing you. Caffeine is a drug, and it interferes with our circadian rhythms. If we drink it at the wrong time, it can affect our sleep patterns. We can become addicted to it as the one thing that brings our cognitive functioning to normal levels if our sleep quality hasn't been up to much. I have a habit of playing a cricket or golf game on my phone when I feel as if my brain is fried. I have a mixed view of it. I think it serves me as a buffer between meetings or tasks, a chance to give my brain a rest. I can decompress by not having to think for a few minutes and just let myself play. This is not altogether a bad thing, and I will espouse the value of play later in the ascent. But I do recognise when it becomes more than a ten-minute filler and decompressor. When I sit down with a cup of coffee and spend an hour playing a Stick Cricket® tournament, I know I have wasted time, and then I beat myself up. I give myself a hard time that I should have been reading something improving, expanding my mind. We all have activities or moments we run to when we need to escape life, and so we should. We just need to make sure we are consciously in control of those habits, rather than allowing them to swallow us up.

**Key Takeaway:** In this ladder step, good habits can wither, and we can pick up bad ones for comfort or immediate reward. Build good habits, such as blocking time for a workout routine. This is a period of change for you and naturally, therefore, your good habits can disappear as you adjust to a new schedule.

## Acceleration Stage Remedies/Tool 6/The Force of Habits

The inspiration for the list of habit tips in the tool comes from the Amazon best-selling book *Atomic Habits* by James Clear. I know of no better book to help you understand why habits form and how to break unhelpful cycles and to build new ones. This is an excellent insight into what drives us as humans—principally, to get rewards to fulfil whatever need we have at that time—and how the habit cycle becomes encoded within us.

Out of an entire book, I distilled down a few points which have been most helpful to me, so I thought I would pass them on. The most important things to remember when wanting to build a new habit are these:

**Instant Reward:** Like seals performing for fish, we will get bored and do something else if our immediate need (or greed) is not met. You need to make sure that you get small rewards for doing something good before you get your bigger rewards later on. For example, I give myself ten minutes of Stick Cricket® if I get a chapter done in this book.

**Path of Least Resistance:** The brain takes the easy way out, so let it take the easy way into a good habit. Making your environment conducive to you doing an activity means you don't need willpower. Put your guitar out on a stand rather than at the back of a wardrobe. Put high sugar/high salt foods at the back of a cupboard rather than on the kitchen worktop. It is amazing just how lazy we are. You will especially find this helpful when you are later in the burnout journey. Get started now.

**Results come later, don't give up:** Like compound interest in a bank account, the chance to bathe in your success only truly comes later. Don't give up now or that reward won't happen. Instead, take the small victories along the way and give yourself little bonuses for keeping going (as per Instant Reward just above).

**Build habits you enjoy:** You won't need to manufacture artificial rewards if you like the habits you have built. If you are one of those twisted people that likes running in sub-zero temperatures pre-dawn, then be my guest. The activity itself is the reward for you.

For the same reasons as in Tool 5 in this chapter, we make change when we agree upon a contract with ourselves. Those are most 'legally' binding when written down. I have repeated the table above so that you can use some Implementation Intention here too.

If you plan to do something, be really specific.

For example, I will do **20 push ups every day in my office** when **I close my laptop before lunch.** Here there is a specific action, a location, exactly when (a trigger action), and who needs to be involved if necessary.

In the same way as you did earlier, use these headings to make sure you are specific in your intentions: describe the action, where it'll happen, when it'll happen, and who it'll happen with (if necessary)

There is so much in this space that I can't condense into a few paragraphs, but you can read the aforementioned *Atomic Habits* as a classical guide on hacking our ability to build unconscious habits … or … you can contact me and ask me about **Mindful Habit Shifting,** a new project for 2025, and a natural follow on from The Burnout Ladder®.

Check out more on www.rightmindfulness.co.uk.

# CHAPTER 8
# RUNG 3: NEGLECT

I went to bed early. I even laid off the wine and closed my laptop down by 8 p.m. Why, then, did I feel absolutely shattered when I woke up this morning, and have remained so throughout the day, even though I had a decent night's sleep? Why am I starting to get irritable and snappy, even at the smallest things?

This is the Neglect step of the ladder. The balance of life is starting to get out of whack. The initial honeymoon period of being able to cope with extra hours and work has now expired. It took an energy boost to get up to speed, and now the body says that it's payback time. But there is a way of maintaining the new norm. Efficiency and effectiveness may have dropped off those initial levels, but there is a way to keep up the output. Throwing more hours at it might get the job done. Even if you are already doing this. Sounds crazy? When you are ascending the Burnout Ladder®, all norms seem to bend out of shape. Neglect is an emotive word and is often associated with a feeling of regret. 'He regretted having neglected his wife.' 'The house had a hopeless air of neglect.' It is the kind of word we use when we wish we hadn't taken something or somebody for granted, and the associated regret is a stubborn and unpleasant emotion. However, when we are on this rung of the ladder, we are most certainly neglecting others and perhaps, more importantly, ourselves. And these moments we are missing in life. We can't ever bring them back.

To maintain this new pace of work and life, we have needed to accelerate. When we press the gas pedal in our cars we burn more fuel. The equivalent action in the body is to release more action-inducing hormones such as adrenaline. When there is more stress, then more of the fight-or-flight hormone cortisol will be released as well. As we know, this in small doses is not harmful, but when persistent over long periods, will send us out of balance and affect our mood regulation. Layer this on top of the fact that we are probably not sleeping so well, then we could become a ticking time bomb each time a cup of tea gets spilled. Concentration is not as good as it was. With so much to do, we need to multitask, which is a fallacy of a concept. It only leads to mistakes when rushing, and with a mind not firing on all cylinders, to not be able to focus on one task will create more. When we multitask, we are actually slicing our time between activities and each time we switch from task A to task B, we lose some information about A, which we then need to pick up when we go back to it. We end up reworking a lot of it because we have become less efficient, making more mistakes as we try to do too much. None of this does anything for our confidence.

The body is starting to tire, and we cannot maintain the pace we had in the Acceleration phase, which means we can't do anything else but increase the hours we are putting in still further. In a non-flexible 24 hours per day, something's got to give. Our workday has become more flexible though, since we start to realise that if we can't do something in the daytime, we have got a safety option to leak into the evenings or the weekends. We are most definitely placing work ahead of ourselves and others. We ignore the things that keep us maintained and healthy. If we were a car, we would not be keeping the tyres inflated or cleaning it inside and out. You would leave it until the last fumes of fuel are in the tank before refilling. (Now, I have often thought of that scenario as a bit of a thrill, seeing if I could cheat the fuel clock, so to speak. But when you do actually run out, it is no fun thing, and it requires more for more resources and energy than merely pulling over at the petrol station for five minutes.)

You are not a car; you are a person. And a person needs a routine of balanced and nourishing activities. You need to work and play, and you need to exercise and stay fit. What's more, you need to enjoy the ride. This is the life you are living right **now**. Do you want it to be all work, or are there moments you are missing too? Did you not make it to a child's sports day or a school play? Did you miss out on a trip to the match with your friends because you felt as if it would take up too much time and a) you needed Saturday to catch up on emails or b) you worried that the inevitable ensuing hangover after post-match drinks would make you less effective the next day and possibly carry over and impact your work performance? Hold onto this thought too, as you will notice this in the Cynicism step of the ladder on the next rung up. Not only will you be missing stuff, but you will also really come to resent missing out on life when the work payback is no longer there.

Are you starting to feel a little pinched? Perhaps things aren't going so well in your project or job, and the world is turning against you. The initial gloss of reward has worn off. The dopamine hit of the extra cash or the status you have achieved has also fizzled out. Where do you turn? To a drink or a cigarette?

## Lacking self-love?

The definition of neglect, as a noun, is 'the state of being uncared for,' (according to Google Oxford Languages, Ref. 27). You are in a position where you have decided to deprioritise your own well-being for the sake of fulfilling a different need, whatever that may be. This may have been subconscious. There is nobody, I hope, who sets out to tear themselves apart at the start of such a journey, but in your heart of hearts, you knew that something would have to give to subsidise this extra effort. Whichever way you dress that up, that is a lack of self-love. It is a lack of self-compassion. If you said you were going to do that to someone else, i.e., deprioritise their health for the sake of them fulfilling more output, they wouldn't feel so great about you, yet here you are doing it to yourself. (And sadly, the reality is that a lot of organisations are either aware of what they are doing to people, or just don't care.)

Self-compassion, by some kind of evolutionary necessity, is one skill we are not so accomplished at. Without hammering the point home yet again, it is the self-critical beings who may survive better than the self-loving ones. If you can see your faults and correct them, then at least in the short term, you will last to fight another day. But what harm are you doing to yourself? It is very easy to get lost in self-recrimination and judgement. It is even easier to perpetuate burnout traps by only thinking of the need to do better, whether it be in work situations, or generally those in life which appear to have gone awry. It is so easy to beat up on ourselves as a motivation to need to do better. We neglect to give ourselves a much-needed congratulatory pat on the back for what we have done right.

Kristin Neff is an associate professor in educational psychology at the University of Texas and she has conducted, over the last couple of decades, some highly insightful research on the benefits of self-compassion. There is an excellent speech she gives, which is available online, about some of the comparisons and contrasts of self-esteem and self-compassion. A client will often come to me and will present that their self-esteem is low. This is more often than not absolutely a right self-diagnosis. It's a symptom, however, of a myriad of causes which are buried deep down in their belief systems and subconscious memories. (i.e., a result of previous experiences or behaviours which have led them to believe their self-worth is low).

An attribute of self-esteem is that we are always comparing ourselves to average. In our Western culture, we have to be better than average to feel any kind of worth in ourselves. As Neff puts it in her talk, (Ref. 20), if anybody told you that you were 'average' at anything, you would be 'crushed'. Your entire system of self-worth depends on you being better than this, of course. Does that mean that those who are not better than average should feel an automatic sense of self-loathing? Self-esteem is outcome-based, which means it is a measure which has arisen from other factors, such as our achievements and failures. And we often attach our happiness to that measure. What is more, it is a self-fulfilling prophecy tending to spiral downwards. If self-esteem is low, we criticise ourselves more, which makes us feel worse, and so the loop continues. We have already discussed how being negative on ourselves tightens our mental muscles, keeps us under a cloud of threat, and therefore, makes us perform less well. What she proposes is a counterattack, and this has become a popular psychological movement, known as self-compassion.

## Would you say that to a friend?

What is self-compassion anyway? At the thought of the words, are you conjuring up magazine images of someone cosying up on the sofa with a steaming cup of coffee, giving themselves a warm hug? It is such a polarising word. There are those who recoil at such namby-pamby self-treatment. There are others who crave some kindness to themselves because that is exactly what they are missing. So often, tears come when people realise just how horrible they have been to themselves, even when they hold everyone together around them.

There are three elements to self-compassion as described by Kristin Neff (Ref. 20).

1. **Treat yourself** *kindly*: This might sound obvious, but in the barrage of our constant threats and self-criticism, it is a habit we often fail to get into. Kindness means encouragement, support, and acceptance of ourselves as who we are; that we are a flawed person, and there is nothing wrong with that. This is flipping the self-talk from constant criticism for failing to live up to standards to, '*I have done my best. I will make mistakes and that's okay.*'

2. **Common humanity**: Going from: '*Am I different from the others and trying to be better than average to manage my self-esteem?*' to: '*I am the same. Yes, we are ALL imperfect.*' Perhaps your own self-compassion can now extend to others and help us to form a connection.

3. **Mindfulness**: More to come on this in this section, but for now, here is a simple message to remember: mindfulness is essentially about being with what is. That is, accepting the present moment, the present us, without questioning it. If we accept that we are suffering, then we can give ourselves compassion. If we are denying

it, then there would be no point, because we wouldn't acknowledge our suffering.

Self-compassion is something I have worked on personally as a priority in recent times. I can definitely endorse the power of giving ourselves some room to breathe and allowing ourselves to be 'us' in a world where judgement is the norm. I feel like it buys us some space to breathe. As in a lot of the individual problems which this book is hoping to solve, self-care can vanish when the pressure is on, and our heads become crowded with self-criticism. We need to *practice* self-compassion, just as any other skill or habit we are attempting to instil, for it will come under real fire when climbing the ladder.

Don't despair. You are really starting to ascend the ladder into dangerous heights here, and this is the first step which doesn't seem like fun at the time. But the tools in this section can revitalise you like no other, and you can shift not only your mood, but your mindset.

## Neglect stage tools

It seems quite intuitive to say that the counter-offensive on neglect should be to nurture, but that is exactly what I am going to prescribe. Here, we go two ways in the remedies. One is to go quiet and still, and the other is to get moving.

Once again, the premise here is not to wait until this stage of the ladder or even be on it at all to set good routines for looking after yourself like this, but if you do find yourself here, experiencing the symptoms I outline, then I offer these suggestions. One of the reasons burnout happens is that we don't realise it is happening to us until we are in it. Which is a bit of a kicker. Imagine if you didn't realise you were being eaten by a snake until it was halfway through swallowing your arm? You would find it much more difficult to extricate yourself. In a sense, burnout is like that (if you can detach yourself from the unpleasantness of the metaphor), but you can save your arm as well as the rest of you.

The core factor of the Neglect stage is that we sacrifice the present for the sake of the future. The extra effort now will come good at some point down the line. An investment in hard work now may result in a promotion later as I build my cache. Even if it is only to pay the next few months' rent, it is a swap of what we live life for—our family, friends, and hobbies—to spend more precious time working.

So, here is a quick summary of all the tools you are about to see. There is a real divide in terms of type of activity, so even within this one rung of the ladder, there is plenty of choice.

1. **Mindfulness:** The gift of being in the present and accepting it for what it is. In this context, this is about not letting the moments slip by. It is also a break from the constant mental chatter inside our heads.

2. **Self-compassion:** As discussed above, it is better to encourage ourselves rather than to

over-criticise. Nurture is the counter to neglect, quite obviously.

3. **Physical exercise:** Everyone is telling you that you look pale and drawn, you're not getting enough time outside, and you can see your belly growing over your belt. Exercise is one of the single best tools for protecting your health and getting you out of a rut.

## Neglect Stage Remedies/Tool 7/ Being in the Now

### The gift of the present

Research has shown that being able to enjoy the present moment makes us happier than any other thought we might be having about past or future. Even if we are reminiscing about our first love or our favourite ever holiday, if we can absorb ourselves in the present moment, then we are at our happiest. It could be watching our team score a winning goal or doing some knitting; if we are sufficiently absorbed in the task so that we are in the Flow Zone (where the challenge of the task perfectly matches our ability to do it), then this is our nirvana. Yet, we spend at least half of our waking lives mentally time-travelling; regretting or replaying the past or anticipating the future. This is not necessarily productive time. It is not learning and moving on, nor planning a day out or a meeting. It is a thought stream which carries us away in a reverie as if we are in a dinghy on a wild river without a paddle to steer, ending up stranded on the rocks time and again.

Being present is to be mindfully aware of what is happening in any given moment. That is to say, the moment you are in now, not the one you experienced ten seconds ago. Right here, right now. It is so tough to do because of the way the mind works by attaching judgement to everything we experience.

Let's say you are mindfully looking at a flower while sitting on a park bench during your lunch hour. You are taking in its details—the colours, the textures of the petals, the intricacies of all its inner parts, the stamen, the pollen. Your mind is totally absorbed. Then, you witness a bee visiting the flower and busily drinking in its nectar. *How wonderful nature is*, you think. Then, a thought crosses your mind. How much of life is like this? Quid pro quo. You don't get anything for nothing, do you? The bee gets its nectar but only because nature has decreed a contract between bees and flowers. There is a transaction taking place. No free lunch. It will carry the pollen to another flower. That's why the bee got it; not through the wonder of nature, but the necessity. Isn't it just the life we all live? We give up our time and energy (and so much more) so we can get money to live—our nectar. Whoever gives me something for nothing … ? Which reminds me, why am I here staring at this bloody flower doing 'nothing' when I have a massive list of things to do? I am behind on that task I said I would do for my colleague. My boss wants me to stand in for her at that meeting this afternoon and I have no idea what to say. What am I doing here when there is so much to do?

There are a billion ways a mind can be taken away from enjoying the present moment, and it is a juggernaut which is hard to stop. The mind likes to crack the whip. It doesn't seem to get the value of stepping back and giving itself a rest. Even though when it does, it responds so well. It is concerned with helping us survive. It will make us think of all the things we need to do which help us to keep turning up in this world.

Sadly, we are wired for survival based on the premise that at any given moment, we could be struck down by a predator or ousted from the tribe. Our amygdala responds to threats, and in the modern world, there are oodles of them (or so it thinks). The less anxious amongst us come to realise that most of the things we worry about were not worth the brain time we gave them, but at the time, the amygdala does not know this. It is just doing its best to protect you, as are all the processes that go on in our threat detection and defence. If we realise this, we can learn to be with it, rather than fight it. It's a marvel, really, if only we choose to look at it that way.

## How to be mindfully aware

How often do you think you are aware? I mean really, truly aware. Not that often, in fact. Awareness is paying attention to the present moment and not judging it. Using your senses to take in the information around you. When looking at the flower on your lunch break, that was awareness ... until the thinking-and-doing mind took over and analysed the situation, creating stories and associations. When using your senses, you were *being*, just allowing yourself to be. There was no agenda other than to pay attention and, perhaps, to marvel and be grateful for what you saw.

Mindfulness is often misunderstood, and adequately and vehemently avoided by some, for fear that they will be taken over by some mystical religious cult. This is sad, as science is repeatedly revealing that the practice of mindful meditation, for instance, is reshaping the brains of people who do it. They become less prone to stress, less reactive, more kind and grateful. More capable of self-compassion. This is neuroscience, not mumbo-jumbo.

So, how do you do this? To be in the moment and mindful is so simple in theory but bloody hard in practice.

## Formal Mindfulness (Meditation)

This is when we sit down (or lie down) and meditate. Google 'mindful meditation' and look for images, we tend to see photos or cartoons of people sitting cross-legged on the floor, perhaps with fingers and thumbs connected in a *mudra* (placing fingers and thumbs together). Already, people are instantly put off. There is a perception that this is how it must be done. It looks so esoteric and exclusively spiritual to many. In fact, the main reason that people are seen to be sitting like this on the floor is because it is a common Eastern custom to do so, and a habit that remains. This practice is thousands of years old and originates from that part of the world.

We can meditate sitting on a chair, on a bus, or standing in a supermarket queue. To formally meditate is to take a step back, focus on something like our breath or a candle to anchor us to the present moment, then mentally observe what is happening in the present moment. Using our senses to hear sounds, the touch of our body where we sit, the feel of our breath as a sensory experience. This, if we allow it, will ultimately quieten the mind to enable us to stop for a few moments and witness the patterns of it. The aim, despite the misunderstanding of so many, is not to *stop* the mind wandering. It is to hold thoughts and feelings in genuine, unfiltered awareness, notice their patterns and then mentally regain control, but with gentleness and self-kindness.

Meditation gives you

a) Increased focus; the ability to remain on task,

b) The ability to see your thoughts/feelings/emotions and their patterns, so that you may become aware of your mental habits and change them if you want to,

c) A sense of grounding and calm—leaving you more relaxed,

d) It has been shown to halve the risk of depression in those who have suffered the most debilitating forms of the illness (Ref. 21). It even reduces the suffering in the experience of physical pain (see the work of Vidyamala Burch I refer to later in this chapter).

e) Much more ... see further reading at the back of the book.

It can be uncomfortable for some but, in my opinion, is suitable for the vast majority of the population. Just because something seems disconcerting at first, does not mean we should not do it. If we are avoiding wanting to see our own thoughts, feelings, and emotions, then that might possibly be the exact reason to do it. But I wouldn't do it alone. Go to a class or see a meditation teacher 1-2-1 who will be able to guide you and encourage you through any challenges. And of course, I am biased because I am a meditation teacher and a practitioner. I use mindfulness all the time as part of an intervention with clients to calm their nervous system so that they may think clearer about their problems. The practice does me personally a great deal of good and I naturally assume it will be good for everyone else too. And if it isn't for you, there are other ways to get your mind calm and to reduce stress.

It is very difficult to get the mind to calm, and people give up because they don't realise that is the point. If there was nothing in our heads, there would be no work to do, no mental muscle to train. The outcome of meditation is usually a calmer mind of course, but the purpose is to be present with it, whatever we experience.

## Informal Mindfulness

If sitting to meditate formally is not your thing, then to practice on the run, so to speak, might be. In many workshops, I have heard delegates say at the end of the day that they would like to practice more mindfulness and that they like the idea of doing it informally. By informal, I mean very simply to do as your teacher might have told you in school:

*Pay attention to what you are doing!*

Quite simple really. Except it's not. For just like trying to sit down and focus on the breath—which seems a mundane activity and hard for the brain to stick with—it is not as easy as it sounds, to pay attention to what we are doing. When we first get out into nature, in the woods, for example, we will draw deep breaths and consider how lucky we are to be able to be amongst all this fresh forest air. Then, after we have taken in what there is to see, hear, smell, and feel, our minds will probably wander off somewhere. We might look at our watch and lament that we only have a short time to enjoy this, feel guilty about being out in nature while others are slaving in the office or with a crying baby at home. A current dispute we are having with someone might crop up in your head, so we think about that. Almost immediately, we are no longer in the woods. We are time-travelling, predicting someone's next move, replaying a conversation, plotting a revenge, fearing receiving a text message which disturbs our peace, even though we are no longer at peace anyway.

Being here in the woods may be absorbing for a few moments and very pleasant if that is our thing. But eventually, our minds will want us to attend to more urgent matters. Just like meditation, we will need a structure or technique to keep anchored in the present moment. If we had constructed a fence, then we would need strong posts to keep the panels in place and not have it blown over in the first strong wind. So it is with mindfulness. Our ability to stay focused on something relatively mundane is compromised unless we have methods to do so, or if we are incredibly experienced at it. I have been meditating for ten years, and yet my mind is often like a pinball, depending on my mood and life situation.

If we play a musical instrument, it is relatively easy to become engrossed in it as long as the piece we are playing is within that Goldilocks Flow Zone boundary of being challenging enough but not too hard for our own abilities. This is because the brain and body are challenged, whereas if we are taking a walk, we probably are interested for a while, but then the thinking-and-doing mind takes over; solving problems in our heads, making plans. We don't need to think about walking, since those neural pathways are so established. This is where we need a structure. I dedicate this tool to the Radio broadcaster Adrian Chiles, who I saw on television recently undertaking a walk around a coastal Yorkshire town, carrying a video camera to record it for us (Ref. 22). He told of his struggles with depression and how he had adapted advice from his therapist on how to take a mindful walk (this could apply to any journey by the way).

## Mindful Walking (20:20:20)

He called it '*20:20:20.*' It goes like this. As you walk or travel, for the first 20 seconds or paces (roughly), look downwards. Look at the ground, its textures and details. If you are walking, how does it feel to walk upon it? How do your feet feel within your shoes? Even better sensorially if you are barefoot! The aim is not to judge, merely to experience. Just be safe while you are walking and watch where you are going. But isn't that the point? To pay attention.

For the next 20 seconds or paces, look more horizontally. Scan around you, making sure if you are walking that you look where you're going if you need to! You may pick out hedges, farm animals, bus stops if you are in a town, or the padlock on a gate. Anything, as long as you notice it.

Then, for the final 20, look upwards (again, being safe …). You might see the sky—interesting cloud patterns or a beautiful blue. If you see nothing but dull grey, notice your reaction to it. Does it make you gloomy? If so, can you think of a time when that sky was clear and blue, and that it will be again? If you are in a city, you might pick out a crane above you, or a treetop or tall building.

Once again, this is just noticing. Letting your senses take in the details of what is actually around you; turning off the workings of the mind lost in a narrative which, most of the time, is not that helpful. I love this structure, and it really helps me get grounded if I go off for a walk and find my thinking-and-doing mind crowding my being for space.

## Pick a colour

Another tip I like that builds your skills of awareness and noticing is to start out a day with a colour in mind. Maybe you pick red. During the day, you would resolve to stop and notice if you see the colour red and what it looks like to you (I mean in terms of senses). I did this a few months ago on a walk, and I could see red on a traffic speed limit sign, the rear light of a car, a red leaf within other green leaves on a tree. All of this helps me detune from toxic thinking and helps me to train my skills of noticing what is around me. Not only do we get the benefit of better mind control, but we also get to see a world which we are missing 99% of the time. And although this was months ago, I can still remember those details which I would have long forgotten consciously, had I not been paying attention. How useful might that be if applied to life in general?

## Why bother with mindfulness?

You may reason that it is pretty much a waste of time to try and sit still for a few minutes and do nothing. We are all programmed, in modern life, to get things done, to achieve. It feels wasteful to sit still. But we have to stop sometimes. We also need to just *be*, as there are so many shown benefits of 'being' like this.

If I gave you a pill that had no side effects or risks that would help you:

- De-stress
- Reduce the chance of depression
- Calm anxiety
- Sleep better
- Reduce suffering (related to any physical or emotional pain)
- Have better relationships
- Improve your creativity
- Improve your kindness to yourself and others
- Make you easier to live with
- Enjoy life more and be generally more content

… would you take it? Of course you would.

This is what mindfulness can do for you. As I have already related, modern life makes our brains so much more susceptible to external threats which are not real, and so we keep our minds and bodies on alert for most of our lives. This fight-or-flight means you can't rest and heal. Neuroscientists have shown that practising mindfulness can make for a calmer and more productive, happy mind. Just a few moments in a day can make a mountain of difference.

**Are you too busy for mindfulness?**

What do you think? The answer nearly always comes back as '*yes.*' Well, maybe you don't have time for a 30-minute meditation before getting the kids up for school, I get that. But remember, all you have to do is pay attention to what you are doing now, so you don't have to break a stride in your day. Noticing what is going on as you do it is all you need to do—taking your shower, brushing your teeth, making a coffee, looking out the window at the sky, driving to work.

As you're getting tired and chronic stress builds up, concentration is wavering. We have already discussed in this chapter that meditation can help our brains to perform better cognitively and rationally, helping us to focus and make better decisions. Also, not everybody wants to sit for long periods of time to be with themselves. It can seem counterintuitive to someone who is plagued by intrusive thoughts, when all they want is distraction from that. They don't want to be made more aware of them. Well, distraction is not the cure for that, but I appreciate it's not for all. To make mindfulness more accessible, we can do this in smaller bites.

Micro-moments of mindfulness can be just as important, if not more so. If you can sprinkle your day with smaller moments of paying attention, you will get your brain to think mindfully more often than perhaps just one burst of meditation which, when done, leaves you ticking a box and then forgetting about it. I am not saying that is what meditation is, but many believe that. They go to their meditation app, dutifully follow a guided meditation for ten minutes, then can't wait to get on with their day and say, 'Yep, done my meditation. Now for my circuits class.' This is not the spirit in which it should be approached, since it is not all about the result, it is also the joy of simply being. That said, even approaching it in that mechanical, tick-box way is better than not doing it at all.

## S-T-O-P

The STOP meditation is as quick or as long as you want it to be. I have been timed in workshops at doing this in 37 seconds, but it could be 10 or 20 minutes if you prefer. The structure goes like this.

You would use this process usually when you feel as if you are encased in an overwhelming brain-freeze of stress. As if your mind was like an electronic device with too many applications open at once. The processor can't handle the sheer amount of multi-tasking it has to do. You are sitting over your laptop, and you haven't stopped working for at least a couple of hours. You don't know what to do next, and the world is collapsing in on you, it seems. So, follow the acronym ...

**S**—Stop, slow down. Sit back in your chair, sitting straight if you can, upright and dignified. Close your eyes.

**T**—Take a breath. Take another one.

**O**—Observe. Notice what your breath feels like. What are the physical sensations? Observe also what's going on in your mind. Whatever it is. Don't judge. Allow it in.

**P**—Proceed. Open your eyes and get on with your day.

It's that simple. I do this when I feel overwhelmed and I'm trying to multitask. The tasks, the thoughts, they all seem to swirl around me so that I can't pick anything out. Then I do this exercise, and I realise that it's all still there in front of me, but it's as if everything has been neatly sorted into order, clarifying exactly what I have to do and when. The purpose behind the meditation is to disentangle from the messy thoughts so they can be seen clearly, and then the next move chosen.

As holocaust survivor and psychotherapist Viktor Frankl said, 'Between stimulus and response, there is a space (Ref. 28).' When we perform activities like STOP—whether for a minute or 20—then we increase the amount of that space. We buy time to respond rather than react and have more chance of avoiding getting caught up in the drama. STOP helps you get back to the reality of the situation rather than the over-wrought narrative you have weaved.

I have included a YouTube recording of the S-T-O-P method to guide you. After a few times, you can just guide yourself I am sure!

# The treasure of pleasure

This is, in a sense, not a purist mindfulness exercise, but I thought it worth introducing. As we get into Neglect phase and then, shortly to come, Cynicism, we really find that life shows us more unpleasantness than pleasantness. Natural negativity biases come into play, and we become gnarly about life in general. Everything we see becomes something that we can growl about. It is almost as if there is a filter over our senses which brings only unhappiness to us.

This next tip or tool I credit to Vidyamala Burch in her book with Danny Penman, *Mindfulness for Health* (Ref. 29). This is an excellent work for helping people with chronic pain. Burch herself suffers with ongoing pain after her innocent involvement in a life-changing car accident where she broke her back and lost the ability to walk. Her way through the suffering which arises is to use mindfulness as a means of accepting her fate and coming to terms what she feels, despite her brain's tendency to dramatize and exaggerate. She also twists the narrative on life by finding what is pleasant, rather than her brain receiving messages which become interpreted as unpleasant. In the body, we tend to listen mostly for signals that something is wrong, the sensations of aches and pains. If we tune in more closely, we find that it is not all this way. Okay, this might sound simple, perhaps even abstract, but it's actually very subtle, and I will give you a few examples which might sound very trivial. The only way for you to understand what this feels like is to try it out for yourself and get into a daily habit.

Here am I, writing this early in the morning and feeling a little jaded and being slightly bothered about my approaching deadlines for getting this book finished. Natural fight-or-flight responses dominate as my neurons fire with motivational messages such as, *'Get on with it!'*, *'You'll never get this done,'* *'You procrastinating moron!'* and *'My back hurts as I sit here all hunched up.'* Not a lot of this is real, perhaps only that I have an aching body. The rest is drama and thought which we know is mostly fiction. So, lets change the narrative.

- Picking up my cup of coffee (which is getting cold, but I won't worry about that), I put my hand around the ceramic mug and feel its smoothness and uniformity—that is pleasant.
- I look outside at some branches on the ash tree in the garden and see just a few of the leaves dancing in the light breeze. That is pleasant too.
- I have a pair of earphones in. I listen to music as I tap away at my keyboard. The light pressure of the earphones becomes comfortable in my ear. That is pleasant. The ends of my fingers tingle as I type. I never really think of that, nor of the clicking sound the keyboard makes as the letters appear. Also, strangely pleasant.
- My bare feet touch the smoothness of the kitchen floor as I sit here. There is a mixture of warmth and coolness on the soles of my feet. That is pleasant.

You see how this works? Taking the mundane and finding the small scraps of pleasure, actively looking for them, I change the conversation in my brain, and all of a sudden, *I am enjoying myself, not enduring.* This is not ignoring the negatives in life, but it is redressing the balance. If I am thinking as I am now, that I am enjoying sitting here writing, then it becomes a reality. I have a stiffness in my back which is sore at this time in the morning, but it is not the main player on the stage now. We are all somewhere along a spectrum of finding the positives in life and some find this more difficult than others. We are naturally geared to ignore the mundanities of life and focus on the big tickets which can hurt us. The threats.

## Savour the moment

In this phase, you are missing moments. And life is a series of them, one after the other. Some are more gravitational than others, that's for sure, but we can learn to find pleasure in a lot of moments that are seemingly mundane. It's yet another tool for turning down the volume on the chatter of the mind. Ironically, a good way to get into the moment is to listen to chatter around you. I remember a family Christmas a few years ago, a typically raucous and noisy gathering. I might normally recoil at the chaos and screeching as everyone clambers over each other to hand out present bags. It is something I have grown to dislike because it's all a bit overstimulating for the senses. Previous to this, I had heard a rugby player talking on a podcast about mindfulness in sport, and he said his way of grounding himself was to use a break in play or a scrum to stop and listen to the crowd. You might expect a player to want to hear the chants of his team's supporters or encouraging shouts to up their game. You might also expect a nervous anticipation of individual abuse from opposition fans, or a dread of them getting their wind up and piling behind their team. None of that; he just listened. He used his senses, and just listened—only for a few moments, as shortly the game would begin again, and he would need to perform, not stand around.

The act gave him two things: once again, the chance to let swirling thoughts and fears settle down and quieten, and the other was simply to appreciate for a second that he was a professional rugby league player at the top of his game, doing something he loved. He just savoured the moment, for a rugby career is over in the blink of an eye, it seems, even if the player is lucky enough to remain relatively injury-free. Not only savouring the experience but this calming of stress also enabled him to return to the game with a clearer mind to think, and with likely more energy.

My Christmas experience was simply to do the same thing, even if the circumstances were totally different. I sat and listened to the noise for a few seconds, as if dissociated from it, watching the scene on TV but being inside the screen. I just listened to the talk, the ripping of wrapping paper, the laughter, the thank you's. I can remember it so vividly now, simply because I allowed my senses to lock in the feelings and the sensory experiences I was having. If I had been locked inside my simulated world on autopilot, I would have a different memory, or possibly not a memory I could recall at all. I might have simply reinforced my belief that it was all a noisy shambles rather than a show of love and kindness in the family. I updated my mental model for the better.

## Mindfulness Summary

I know many of you will have skipped over this last section, but I am not giving up. Don't just think of mindfulness as a way of trying to sit still for ten minutes when your mind is racing, and you can't wait to get on with your day. Instead, use it as an opportunity to notice the world as it is, in all of its infinite detail, and subtly see how it shifts in balance. Notice what is unreal, imagined fiction, and simply allow the more pleasant non-fiction to emerge. See how you start to accept the moment you are in, rather than resist it, and see how you face situations with calm and poise.

Summary of Tools for Being in the Now (Tool 7)

- Mindful Meditation
- Mindful Walking (20:20:20)
- Pick a Colour
- S-T-O-P
- The Treasure of Pleasure
- Savour the Moment

There are plenty for you to have a go at.

## Self-compassion tools

Full disclosure. This is not an area I am most comfortable with since, like most of us, I seem to love the opportunity of having a go at myself mentally. I know, because of what I have learned, that it is natural to veer towards self-flagellation as a means to motivate myself, but I am also discovering that my survival depends on looking at the other side of the coin. As I get older, I realise that I make more mistakes, some of them I don't even realise I had made until much later in life when I look back. Imagine you are carrying a rucksack on your back through your life, and every now and again, a rock or a small boulder gets loaded into it. These represent your interpretation of the big mistakes you feel you have made in your life. Now you carry that extra weight on your back forever and it doesn't get lighter, only heavier as you add more blame to your burden. No wonder we end our lives stooped over and in pain. This is happening to me—more mentally than physically—as I get older, but I am no different to anyone else I know. I know I have made mistakes and will continue to do so, but as we discussed in Perfectionism way back on the Ignition rung, we need to switch up our thinking on these so as to lighten the load.

To practice self-compassion, you will need to use some kinder words for yourself. I can't feel bad for everything, and I must pick my battles as well as accept fault for some things I have done wrong. But after the acceptance of mistakes, must come the acceptance of self. We are all just trying to make our way. Stuff gets broken, even more so as we get older, and life somehow weaves itself into a tangle.

## Neglect Stage Remedies/Tool 8/ Accept Yourself

In this tool, I have listed pairs of words, which happen to be antonyms. You will see that the ones on the left of each line represent something we may like to think of as desirable (positive) attributes, and their partners are words we probably wouldn't like used about us (negative). (Ref. 30).

Go through this list and circle whichever **negative** attributes you think are most relevant to you. Then prioritise the five which are the most *you*, as you see it. When you have done this, read on below to complete the exercise.

Optimistic | Pessimistic
Confident | Insecure
Kind | Cruel
Patient | Impatient
Honest | Dishonest
Reliable | Unreliable
Creative | Uncreative
Determined | Undetermined
Empathetic | Unempathetic
Generous | Stingy
Intelligent | Unintelligent

Ambitious | Lazy
Compassionate | Indifferent
Curious | Uncurious
Humble | Arrogant
Loyal | Disloyal
Open-minded | Close-minded
Self-disciplined | Impulsive
Adaptable | Rigid
Problem-solving | Ineffective
Organized | Disorganized
Adventurous | Cautious

| | |
|---|---|
| Perseverant \| Quitting | Leadership \| Followership |
| Resilient \| Fragile | Technical \| Non-technical |
| Strong \| Weak | Analytical \| Intuitive |
| Talented \| Untalented | Proactive \| Reactive |
| Trustworthy \| Untrustworthy | Witty \| Humourless |
| Outgoing \| Introverted | Communicative \| Incommunicative |

Now you have identified some characteristics about yourself that you may not be entirely happy with. Normally in these kinds of exercises, you are asked to identify your most positive strengths so that we may work to build upon them. There is a place for that for sure, but this is not about building strength. This is about acceptance of yourself. Taking all the warts and all and beginning to accept them as a part of you so that you may begin to look upon yourself with more kindness. If you had a friend who was suffering with depression, or constantly limped with a sore foot, or had been left by their partner, you would show compassion for them, wouldn't you? You would wish none of these on anyone you know, and probably least of all yourself. Showing kindness for ourselves, however, is the most difficult effort of all.

So, here are the three self-compassion factors that Kristin Neff discussed (Ref. 20). I would like you to take each one of your so-called 'negative' attributes that you have chosen as being most relevant to yourself and follow the instructions below.

1. **Be kind to yourself.**

   Thinking of each attribute in turn, can you turn the script from: 'This is me and it's terrible; I hate myself,' to: 'This is part of who I am, and I am okay with it. I accept myself for this because I know this does not need to define me. If I am a (procrastinator; this is an example word—insert your own here), then there may be good reasons for that. I will work on improving this or making it into a positive force. I am okay with this being part of me. Things will always get better.'

2. **Common humanity.**

   I am just like all of humanity. Flawed and struggling to make my way in the world. I am no better or no worse. I want to be a better person, but I accept that it is not a race. I have my own path to follow, but I understand that I am connected to the whole world through a shared sense of humanity. We are all trying to improve ourselves, but my characteristics are part of who I am as an individual.

3. **Mindfulness.**

   Take the five words you have identified. Remember, mindfulness is about accepting what is. So, accept them if you can. You have called these out after all, so maybe it's not that difficult to do that part.

   I have put in a small recording here so that you can do this exercise, as I know you can't read the print with your eyes closed! But here is the script for you to think about afterwards.

## Accept Yourself

*Now close your eyes and think of the words. Take a couple of breaths and let the words swirl around you in your mind's eye. Perhaps it's not the words you can visualise. It might be images or scenes, real or imagined, that you play out with the feeling of the words, but now in pictures or some other sense. Perhaps you can hear someone saying these words to you. Be with them. Sit and listen, sit and wait. Are these words in isolation really you, or is there some other part of the story? Imagine you are the hero in your own story. Are you only including the chapters in your book that are the most painful for you in the plot? Where are the triumphs? Where are the heroics? You are more than these words, and are they really real after all? How much of this is factual, now that you put them under a mindful microscope?*

I deliberately asked you to isolate these words so that you could label them and call them out (like the faulty thinking categories exercise we covered on the Acceleration rung). Often, we bury our worst fears about ourselves and they grow like a fungus, unseen. They become part of our belief systems which then drives our behaviour. We make corrections for a fault, which sometimes is not really there. This is why I asked you to use mindfulness on the attributes, because it asks, 'What is really going on? What is there, rather than what do I *think* is there?'

It doesn't matter which of Neff's three self-compassion criteria ring true with you. It only needs one spark of fire here to get you thinking about yourself in a different way. You can do it. Just be kinder to yourself, and see the benefits unfold.

## Neglect Stage Remedies/Tool 9/Get Moving

We are designed for moving. One of the things I have learned as I get older is that the longer I sit still, the stiffer I become in my bones. Physical exercise most definitely IS the panacea to a number of health problems, both in body and in mind. Yet it is one of those habits that we so easily let go when we are tight for time, not least because, usually, performing some physical exercise takes time. If you want to go for a half hour run in your lunch hour, then you have five minutes to get ready, longer if you can't find some socks. After the run, you then need to warm down and then take a shower and get dressed back into your civvies so you can wolf a sandwich down on your first call of the afternoon. After predicting how this will make you feel, you often decide to skip it. Too busy anyway. But what we somehow fail to predict is the true feeling we will get afterwards, which is the effect of the endorphins (a natural painkiller which has been naturally selected as a useful aid to make you feel good about exercise so that you will keep running away from danger even when your muscles are screaming), which then leaves you with a residual feeling of bliss and reward. Time is an excuse, but also, the thought of the pain before the joy might put you off too.

A sedentary lifestyle is a killer, but also a recipe for lack of well-being. And have you ever regretted getting up and doing something, even though you didn't feel like doing it? Frankly, I am not going to go on at length here, because it is obvious that moving is how we were built and the brain rewards us for doing so (unless we get injured, of course) with feel-good chemicals. However, it's worth noting that at this stage of the ladder, neglect has kicked in. To exercise is to reverse that neglect. Take care of your body in whatever way you see fit. I don't talk of diet in the ladder, but perhaps you can sneak in a healthy regime here too, as exercise and good diet tend to go hand in hand. Time away from your desk will restore some balance.

Always speak to your doctor before embarking on a new exercise programme though, especially if you haven't done anything for a while or have any existing injuries. There are great programmes out there to ease you into exercise again. I hadn't run for years, until I tried the National Health Service *Couch to 5K* app. Slowly building up resilience and fitness over eight weeks, rather than just going out and trying to hammer out the full distance, gave me the best chance to reach the landmark distance running without stopping. And I did it too. It gave me a sense of achievement, was something I was personally proud of, and it also got me out in nature a few days a week.

## Don't miss your life

Seriously, this rung of the ladder is perhaps the most painful, because we lose sight of what is important for us. Life is a series of connected moments, and sometimes we miss the key ones, which go by in a flash. This is the stage where we start to lose our sense of identity and relinquish that person to our duties. The reason I chose these tools for this stage was that by using them we reconnect with who we are, have a sense of self-respect, and make sure we keep balance of mind and body. By doing that, we are also taking care of those close by who depend on us for support.

# CHAPTER 9
# RUNG 4: CYNICISM

I break away from the tedious PowerPoint presentation I am putting together, focusing, of course, on the massively important font sizes and precise alignment of images and text. I am tired. Another evening of work last night to try and keep the pace has left me without decent sleep and feeling exhausted today. I am feeling agitated as my emails must be piling up while I am wasting my time on this presentation. I am predicting there are probably a few mistakes in there, even though I can't be bothered to check. I have put together some shoddy work of late, and doubtless I am going to get some rebukes and rebuffs for my sloppiness. I am mildly (but only mildly, mind you) regretting a lack of patience I showed to one of my team, who couldn't seem to understand that I don't live in their world every day, and that they really should provide me with context before reporting an issue to me. My problems are bigger than theirs, after all, but perhaps I now regret snapping at them. I open an email with dread. It is a high energy email from our functional VP praising everyone for their hard work in achieving our quarterly results, but we must redouble our efforts for a challenging quarter ahead in which we face several head winds … etc., etc. My cursor hovers over the 'close window' button and I slap my finger down on the mousepad. *How nice it must be to live in YOUR world!* I get up and go to the coffee station, realise it's broken, huff my contempt, then go back to my desk, put on my coat, and walk out of the building for some fresh air. I bump into another disgruntled colleague. Great, a perfect opportunity to offload with a good moan … I'm such a horrible person.

If you hadn't guessed from the chapter title or my undoubted crankiness, I have hit the Cynicism rung of the ladder. I must have ignored my signs of stress and fatigue which had hit me in Neglect phase, and my general grouchiness has shown its teeth. I am seemingly at the end of my tether, although at this stage I do still have some fight left in me, an almost rebellious streak and a glint in my eye. I might be full of stress, trying to multitask (but ineffectively). Starting jobs or mini projects in desperation to get some motivation back, getting discouraged and giving up, I have a mound of initiatives left abandoned or barely started. How did I get here? What happened to all that optimism back in Ignition and Acceleration? What is the matter with me? Why am I so snappy with people? I don't even seem to care about their issues, even if I have created them with my incompetence.

There's a lot going on here. In some respects, this rung of the ladder holds the most ambiguities and contradictions. I have some fight in me, as I did back further down. But this time, the energy is being channelled slightly differently. When disappointments happen, it is easy to recoil, to tense up and avoid rather than approach. Our natural responses to threat are aroused, and we go into fight-or-flight mode. This is fine when there are real fights to be had, or we can actually run away. Most of the time, when it is boiled down, we have a few problems which need to be solved, no different from any other work situation. The difference is that if we shut down now and go in with a cynical or resentful approach, our brain's aversion pathways will fire, and we will be very closed off and not so creative about how we handle these issues. That is also why the mind and body tools from the last chapter are so important, as they will improve our mood and allow us to approach rather than avoid. We may still have that fight, but we are not making the most of our own internal resources.

But here we are: feeling negative, lacking passion for the job, lacking faith in ourselves, and letting the inner critic walk over us. Our chronic stress and exhaustion cause faulty thinking, and negative emotions dictate our thought streams. The more tired we get, inducing unpleasant feelings in the body, the more our cynicism turns into a lack of confidence in ourselves. We go into a downward spiral of self-recrimination, indecision, and inaction. Our cynicism is driven by an excessive stress response which leads to anxiety and self-doubt. (A side note here. As I was editing and re-writing this book, I have been burning the oil to meet publishing deadlines. Old hang-ups and self-doubts have reared their heads once again. I found that the more I got tired and worn down, then the more I would take entire passages out altogether, with a flourish of the red pen. I hated hearing my own voice on the page more and more, and yet when I had started out, I was enjoying the process and making only minor tweaks here and there. The irony is not lost that I have been climbing my own ladder, and Cynicism is definitely where I have got to! Don't worry, I am over it now, but it also shows just how quickly this stage of burnout can take over.)

## A little love goes a long way

There are a few recurring themes in this stage. Your chronic stress results in you running on a short fuse, making mistakes as you try to keep up but also lacking care for your work, even if you are (or were) a perfectionist; you just don't care now. You will keep on experiencing this if you climb further up the ladder. But the most worrying factor is your lack of kindness—for others and yourself.

In the previous chapter we discussed self-compassion. Now I am talking about that shown to others. There was a movement born in the 1990s out of a difficult period of violence in the San Francisco Bay Area, when an exasperated person mused that, instead of the media reporting on 'random acts of violence,' could they focus for once on 'random acts of *kindness*'? This, of course, has become a foundation and a widespread concept, and there is even a set day (although there seems to be a day for everything now) each year on 17 February. 'Random acts' means doing something unexpected. It will certainly be so for the recipient, and if you mix it up in terms of the type of kindness you show, then you might surprise yourself too. You can find out more from the Random Acts of Kindness organisation (Ref. 23) on how to practice kindness more.

Why does this matter? Simply because showing kindness is one of the best things we can do for our general well-being and state of contentment. When we feel low, a major factor is the lack of presence of a neurochemical called *serotonin*. It acts as a neurotransmitter, which means it either speeds up or blocks messages in brain and body. It has several functions in the body, but one of them is to regulate mood. If we are lacking serotonin in the body, then we can experience anxiety and/or depression. Showing kindness encourages serotonin production, even more so than receiving it.

Showing kindness also boosts another neurotransmitter called *dopamine*, which has a part to play in our motivation levels and reward pathways in the brain. In fact, kindness is a gift which keeps on giving, because it also boosts *oxytocin*, which is sometimes known as the 'love' or 'cuddle' hormone. We are social animals by natural selection, so evolution has favoured us being nice to each other by releasing little bursts of feel-good in the form of oxytocin. Kindness also reduces stress, leaving us calmer and more content. So, there is quite a shift in our hormonal cocktails, leaning towards feeling better.

On a very basic level, I feel that if we are thinking

a kind thought, it is impossible to be chewing over an unkind one. When we think of someone who we know and judgement takes over, and we may be thinking unkindly towards them because they are not showing us the love we think we deserve (I hope this isn't just me), then there is an antidote. Think the opposite. If you think they are angry with you for no other reason than they haven't contacted you lately and this stimulates your defences to call to mind all the times they annoyed you, prompting unkind thoughts, then do the opposite. Think of all the times they amused you, helped you, supported you, lifted you. (If you can't think of anything, then ask yourself if it is a bad thing that you are not in contact! Seriously. We need people, but we need people who are doing us good—but definitely try the kind thought route first.) Maybe they are going through tough times. Maybe they are ill. God knows they have enough going on in their own lives without spending all their time worrying about you. This is Egocentric Thinking, remember? Spare a kindly thought that they are doing their best in life, just like you. Break the silence by sending them a text, with no hidden agenda, merely to ask how they are doing. Or do one of a myriad of random acts of kindness ideas on https://www.randomactsofkindness. org/kindness-ideas.

## Show a little gratitude

If there is one element of the human condition that I find the most desolate, it is our inability to remain grateful for what we have. It is, of course, that fundamental natural characteristic which drives us on to be successful. Not settling for what we have, to be better, to compete, to strive, is a necessary part of progress. But what we have available to us right now is quite wondrous. Our planet is beautiful to look at, with magnificent colours which we can see (and created) thanks to the intricate mechanics of our eyes. As I write this, I am sat in a relatively comfortable yet spacious kitchen, safely behind glass and brick, protected from the beastly hurricane which is raging outside. It is 05:30 a.m. in the morning, and the reason I am here this early is because the wind was keeping me awake, stirring up anxious thoughts about my week to come and how much work I must do. I wasn't thinking how grateful I was to be in a warm bed, safe and sound. I could have been grateful for the builders' skill in putting together a wind-proof house, for the designers and manufacturers of my comfortable mattress and my toasty duvet. I could also be grateful to myself for providing the necessary funds to keep all this protection around me. No, our minds don't work like that. Like a hungry dog that has snaffled up a treat, all that has gone before has been banked and we want something else. These home comforts are a part of life and have been for a hundred years. My hunter-gatherer ancestors might have been very grateful for my luxuries. (Or would they? They may not have been kept up half the night worrying about the work they had to do to get them in the first place.)

The point is: gratitude gives us those chemical boosts that we get from kindness and self-compassion. It lifts us and makes our brain work better, holding anxiety and low mood at bay. It is unnatural to simply be grateful, especially when we introduce our natural competitiveness into the mix. We might enjoy our kitchen, but as soon as we go to someone else's house and see a bigger and better one, then any gratitude we had might naturally fade. That's because we are programmed to go after what they have to avoid being left behind. To settle for what we have and be happy about it is swimming against the tide of human progress, but it will certainly lift us in the end.

## Cynicism Stage Remedies/Tool 10/Gratitude

Gratitude—on the Cynicism rung of the ladder, you really need some positive doses of feel-good. You are more likely to be spitting out expletives and resenting those around you. I know of few better ways to stem the tide of unhappiness that swamps over us than to think a grateful thought. Again, we can only really place our attention on one thing at a time, so the happy and contented thought crowds out the unwelcome ones. It will also help ground us so that we can remember that it doesn't take a lot to make us happy sometimes, and that maybe what we are reaching for just isn't worth it.

A simple tool: I recommend you start each day with a gratitude thought.

Now, I know this is very difficult to do to start with. People who try this often come back with the response that it gets boring after a few days. Once they have said they are grateful for their happy childhood, their partner, or their kids, then the well has pretty much dried up. But this is the point. These are the big things in life. And there are infinite possibilities of smaller circumstances, events, and things to be grateful for too. You may even tire of praising your warm cup of coffee, but how about the people who made it? The coffee farmer, the pickers, the manufacturers, the supply chain, the truck driver, the retailer. You could dive into any of these details for just about anything you want to focus on. The idea is that you think only of one thing a day, and it is starting out with that mindset that might tilt you away from cynicism, even just to give you a short break.

## Cynicism Stage Remedies/Tool 11/ Be Your Biggest Fan

Aligned to the idea that we are own worst critic and that some self-compassion won't hurt, this tool is designed to tilt your view of yourself back to the positive. We know that we have more negative thoughts than positive as an evolutionary design feature. We also know that can weigh us down somewhat and make us think we have threats which aren't real. Much like self-compassion, it is the hardest thing for most of us to tell ourselves that we are worthy and have useful skills. We are so programmed to focus on the gap between us and perfect, that we don't consider what has got us this far in the first place.

So, this is really very simple.

**Write down five things about yourself that you like.** Let yourself be self-indulgent, even if you have to remain somewhat accurate. You can't say you're a great swimmer if you can barely cover a length of the pool. And to be honest, I am talking about your softer skills anyway. You could be kind, a good listener, patient, like to laugh a lot. You might be witty and sharp of mind (when you're not on the Cynicism rung anyway) or have a way with people. You could be open-minded, creative, even be reasonably intelligent ... there are lots to go at.

Then, to make sure you are balanced and don't become an egotistical maniac, **think about three things about yourself that you would like to work on.** Don't say you're bad at them; these are just characteristics that you can work on. Nobody is, or shouldn't be at any rate, perfect. Are you a worrier or stress-y? Are you forgetful, maybe not great at remembering people's names? Are you overly fastidious, maybe a little cautious? Again, you know yourself, so think about what you would like to improve. This exercise might just a) jolt you into feeling better about yourself rather than being overly self-critical, or b) give you an incentive to tackle some long-standing niggles you have with your own psyche.

You may of course use some of those attributes from the previous chapter from the tool **Accept Yourself.** Just because you can be okay with something you are not particularly proud of, it doesn't mean that you can't try and improve on it.

## There, there, you're being emotional

Have you noticed your emotions are becoming ragged too at this stage? Perhaps some anger and jealousy.

Flying off the handle frequently, and having a shortened fuse? Because of the constant stress, the brain is reacting more emotionally in the moment, and this leads to more self-beratement and a lack of confidence.

We have a range of emotions. The problem is we only want to have the good ones such as happiness, joy, pride, amusement, serenity. We don't want anger, jealousy, hate, shame, guilt, disgust. We are hedonistic, pleasure-seeking creatures after all. However, if we only desire to feel good, then we do all we can to cling on to those feelings and actively push away the bad. The net result being that we live life defensively, trying to avoid feeling bad and dreading it, which leads to anxiety. Don't believe me? Think of your feelings on a Sunday, the day before the dreaded Monday morning. You wake up and relish the thought of a Sunday breakfast and a cup of coffee, perhaps read your book or the paper. Then, as time moves on towards noon, you start to clock-watch. Time is speeding up. Soon, it will be late afternoon, then evening, and before you know it, it will be bedtime, a night of disturbed sleep, and then waking up bedraggled for another week on the hamster wheel. (I heard someone describe this whole phenomenon as 'the creeping sadness of a Sunday,' which I thought was so on the money.) The joys of Friday night and the stretching bliss of Saturday are behind you, and reality of life kicks in. There is such a stark contrast between the feelings of each that it is normal to want to yearn for the good feelings and kick away the bad. All of this leads to a closing off—an avoidance of the Monday feeling, which then triggers negative thinking and a lack of creativity and openness to an experience which, let's face it, is rarely as bad as we had predicted.

If you would like further reading on the impact that our feelings and emotions can have on us, then I would point you to the excellent and eye-opening book *Emotional* by Leonard Mlodinow (Ref. 31), which highlights the neuroscience involved in emotions. I will give it a little précis here, as I think there are some key takeaways which can be gamechangers in how we think about our emotions.

We talk about feelings and emotions and use the terms interchangeably. I like to define it all this way as I think it helps us make sense of a highly confusing matter! An emotion is a complex mixture of thoughts and feelings. We think with our heads and feel with our bodies. Recall a time when you *felt* something, such as being in love, or the opposite of that joy, getting dumped. You may remember that the 'feeling' was something in your body, usually a racing heart or butterflies. We even use this terminology in our language, such as, 'I felt sick to my stomach,' or 'I could feel my chest tighten.' The brain is for thinking and the body is for feeling. We have primal systems within us that monitor our environment for safety or danger signals. The *autonomic nervous system* (ANS) is one such regulator. The ANS is responsible for processes in the body over which we appear to have no direct control. That means that while we can control whether we move an arm via messages through the *central nervous system* from the motor cortex, our kidney function, for example, is controlled by an automatic—or autonomous—system.

We are consciously oblivious to it, and what it does, but it is responsible for many of our bodies' essential systems such as heart rate, blood pressure, perspiration, breathing rate.

The ANS detects danger and will, just like the amygdala (see Chapter 2: Causes of Burnout), raise holy hell if it doesn't feel safe. The sympathetic nervous response is the fight-or-flight branch of this system, and it knows how you feel before you do. That is to say, these feelings are unconscious. We don't know about them until our brain has consciously processed all of the inputs.

Our ANS is picking up signals all the time, monitoring the environment for danger. All animals have one. Let's say we walk into a room and there is someone in there we don't know. Our ANS analyses the situation: is this an aggressive-looking person? Could they do us harm? Are we safe here? It feeds this information up to the brain, which then pulls in other data sources from its memory banks. Have we seen this person before, or someone like them? Have we been in this position before? Is it dangerous? How else are we feeling? Tired, worried, anxious? All these feelings happen so quick, and they are out of our conscious control. The brain chooses a reaction based on the sum of these unconscious inputs, then it will decide a conscious action. It could be, for example, to reach out a hand and introduce ourselves to the other person, or it might get us to turn around and walk out of the room. Much will depend on how we were feeling.

This can be explained in Figure 6 below.

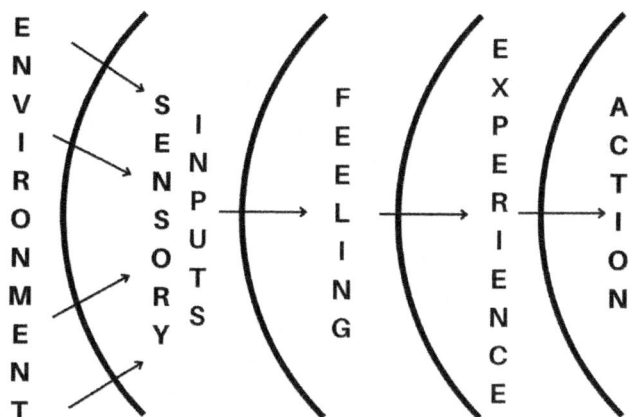

*Figure 6. Filters of Inputs*

This shows how we crunch complex calculations for how we think and act based on how we filter our inputs. We take information in from our external environment, sensory information such as from our five main senses, monitor how we are feeling (sometimes called the *feeling tone*), and layer on this any past experiences regarding this situation that we might have stored in our memory. Out of this sausage machine of rapidly processed data comes a thought, an emotion, or an action. Perhaps all of those.

If we had just had good news about a potential promotion, we might swagger over and introduce ourselves with a flashing smile and a firm handshake. If we were hungry and nervous about our presentation, we might just nervously say 'hi' and then start looking at our phone to avoid any further contact. We are complicated animals. The possibilities in this simplified scenario seem almost countless, so think how unpredictable we can be in even more complex circumstances. What might seem intuitive when mentioned like this is easily forgotten when rationalising behaviours—in ourselves and others. Take this other example. This morning, as I mentioned earlier in this chapter, I was awake early due to a noisy wind outside and my own busy thoughts. When I was eventually up and about, the tiredness I *felt* knocked me back when I started thinking about a work problem, and my general feeling about the week ahead. I decided to go for a hot shower and when I did, I felt totally rejuvenated and refreshed afterwards. I sat and thought again about what was in front of me. My feeling was completely different, and what was originally trepidation became excitement. The hot water and the feel-good impact of getting clean and taking a few minutes out for routine maintenance had reassured my body that I was okay. This gets fed into the computer of my brain and out pops a much more optimistic outlook and a creative and open-minded take on what lies ahead of me.

This is obvious, right? Well, maybe. The insight for me is that our thinking is always guided by our feelings, whether good or bad. If in turn, my thinking is set off on the wrong track, then that will lead to further problems. You can't help your feelings, but you can help your emotions, or at least guide them when you feel they are letting you down.

# FEELING + THOUGHT = EMOTION

This needs some careful reading and reviewing, as it is very possible to misinterpret what I am saying. Even I get confused with this sometimes. Our feelings are something visceral inside of our bodies. They are part of our ANS, which gives us a sense of how we interpret external safety or danger, which then triggers a response. Very simply, we can call this either a fight-or-flight reaction (the sympathetic nervous system response; the word deriving from *sympathos* in Greek—'with emotions'), or it could be called a rest-and-digest state (the *parasympathetic* nervous system response; I like to think of this word as a '*para*-chuting' to safety). This feeling will be fed back to the brain to form part of those mental calculations, but often, they are so quick that our reaction is reflexive. Quick! Danger! Do something. If I am attacked physically, I probably won't have time to think. The ANS response is so quick that I will start lashing out with punches immediately. I won't stop to think, 'Okay—first a left hook, then a right uppercut …'

Often, in dealing with non-life-threatening situations, we do have time, but that, of course, is a variable. Again, this is most easily demonstrated with an example that we all can relate to.

We receive an email from a boss or colleague which criticises us or just plainly triggers us. Whatever it is, it has got us riled! A visceral reaction is triggered. The ANS feels unsafe, under attack. Very quickly after this, the amygdala joins in. *Fight!* Feedback loops between body (in which the heart is already racing, and the veins are thumping in the head as the red mist rises) and mind reinforce the danger signal. We are in red alert. Heart pumping, blood pressure rising, blood sugar increased. What has happened here is that the FEELING was first encountered, and then THOUGHTS were developed as a response, since thoughts are guided by feelings (the thoughts might transpire in words such as, 'I hate you,' 'What do you know?', or often less printable ...). The combination leads to a product called an EMOTION, which in this case could be labelled as anger or rage. The strong feeling gave rise to what we might call an emotional thought, and its power is considerable.

## No time to walk away?

This is where the time factor is vital. It is not the requirement to reply to the email immediately upon reading, so instead, you actually have time to digest it and then act. What happens, of course, is that we are so outraged, we must act now, since this could be a matter of urgency and survival as far as the amygdala and ANS knows, so we press reply and start hammering the keyboard with a response while our hearts are still thumping. As another part of the brain, namely the *Pre-Frontal Cortex* (PFC), responsible for self-regulation and generally behaving like a sensible older brother, joins in the debate, we start to get the feeling that this reaction is something we could regret. We tap at the delete key until our angry words disappear and might even experience relief that we did not act on the reaction. We had time to consider our response, and now that we have, we take a different and probably more diplomatic path. Nobody ever regretted walking away from their computer after receiving an email which pissed them off!

Sadly, in life, we live in real-time, and our responses happen in the moment. We can't help feelings. If someone confronts us, betrays us, irritates us, or antagonises us, we cannot deny these feelings and they cause us to act straight away. How can it be our fault after all these millions of years of evolution? The immediacy and genius of our evolutionary fight-or-flight system drives us to leap in feet first.

## Accept the moment, not your situation

We have done it many times, and we will continue to do it until we die. We will react emotionally occasionally, even if we can achieve constant Zen-line states for most of our lives. The reflexes are too deep. Acceptance of being human and that we are at the mercy of feelings is key, so when it comes to a point where we have acted on them and then regretted it, then we shouldn't berate ourselves. If we accept human feelings and emotions, then we stop resisting. We create additional anxiety around the event even though we can do nothing about our reaction.

Let's say you are driving a car, and you are in a situation where another driver pulled out in front of you and almost (but didn't) cause an accident. They were clearly negligent and at fault. You are angry! You are driving behind them and gesticulating wildly, hoping they can see you in their mirror. Offensive words escape your mouth. You want them to know just what an idiot they are. They don't seem to respond to you. They have just casually come out of a junction, almost killed you, and they are not even aware! Your red mist has descended. Your heart is pumping, and your head feels like it's going to explode. You are so close behind them so as not to be ignored, so much so that who is the dangerous driver now? They come to a set of lights and stop, and you pull up too, close in behind them. You are glaring at the driver through his rearview mirror. They open their door and get out, and they seem to be carrying something resembling a baseball bat. Looking aggressive, they walk slowly to your vehicle. *Oh dear ... I wish I wasn't here now ...*[1]

What has happened is your fight-or-flight defences have reacted, even though the original incident wasn't especially dangerous. But don't forget, your poor amygdala doesn't know that. It just sounded the alarm, and because you might have had a lousy morning—dropping an egg on the kitchen floor, having a client cancel an appointment, a minor tiff with your significant other—your ANS is not feeling too chipper. So, your brain's calculated reaction was over the top, based on some unpleasant feelings and, interestingly, nothing to do with the current incident. The PFC tried to smooth things over, but the strong emotions were just too

1. The reason our hearts still race after a near-miss in the car is because we don't switch off the internal alarms immediately after danger in case there might be another one along in a minute—quite useful having just encountered a snake in the jungle, as it is probable there are more about!

vociferous, and a poor reaction resulted. Hopefully, you managed to extricate yourself from a now genuine threat, and if you did, the emotions might live on within you for a few days—anger may still linger, but now topped up with a measure of regret and shame. A rather unhealthy cocktail which keeps you reliving the experience.

That said, the brain is complicated and tends to avoid pain and pursue pleasure, so your conscious mind may well push away the feelings and emotions you are experiencing. It tries to block them, but the feelings still hang around under the surface, driving our behaviour as long as they do. If you explain your situation, a friend will tell you to move on from it. Just let it go, will you? Easier said than done. Is letting it go denying it, or is it processing the emotion, letting it pass through you? Mostly when people tell others to let something go, they really mean 'just forget about it and move on.' In other words, deny it ever happened and get on with it. Denial rarely helps, and there is a lot of evidence to show that emotions which are not allowed to pass through us can make us ill. (For further information and reading on this, I recommend two authors: Bessel van der Kolk, MD, a psychiatrist and leading expert on trauma therapy; and Dr Gabor Maté, a Canadian physician, also a leading thinker on effects of trauma. See Recommended Reading.)

## How do I process an emotion?

I am glad you asked that because in all my training and reading, I have very often got quite annoyed at vague words to describe something so important. What the hell does *process* mean anyway? Is there some sort of meat grinder in my mind that minces up the contents and turns it into something new?

Here is my layman's view on processing, or letting go of, an emotion. Our emotions (the feeling element) are like strings of electrical impulses passing through the body. Therefore, we feel them in the body as is this is where they occur. Our brain's make sense of them by both of its hemispheres working together—the left side being the logical rational side and the language centre, and the right side being our imagination, images, and feelings you can't quite get hold of. When we 'process' an emotion, we allow both sides of the brain to talk to each other and allow the emotion out of us. It has travelled through the body and out through the brain. A bit like toothpaste being squeezed from a tube. Sometimes this right-left communication doesn't work so well, as in the case of trauma (Ref. 35, Bessel van der Kolk) and the emotion gets stuck in a loop. It is as if the body is reliving it time and again, keeping the body in fight-or-flight even though the danger has passed.

For more regular, yet still disturbing, life events, such as regretting a road rage incident, or feeling jealous about a colleague's promotion and how it made you react to them, then I propose the **Emotions, Truth, Choices (ETC) model.** I first learned about this through a friend, who had come to use it himself and was working on it with his eleven-year-old son who, like most kids, could fly off the handle then agonise inwardly about it later. As a model, it follows a logical path of Emotion coming first, then Truth (or a more rationalised view of the event), and finally Choices—to give us the realisation that there is always a way forward, even if it is to do nothing except learn and move on. Right brain and left brain talking together.

## Cynicism Stage Remedies/Tool 12/ Emotions, Truth, Choices

Although hopefully we accept that having negative emotions is part of the human condition, we still don't want to be labelled as 'emotional'. We often apologise to others for showing emotion. We don't want them to dominate us, but if we are forced to live with them, we may as well make them our friends.

It is also interesting to know that we are to a certain extent at the mercy of our 'feeling' and we should definitely tune in to it to understand when we might be at our best or otherwise. It is better for a 'hangry' sufferer like me, not to make big decisions just before lunchtime. I am a big advocate of acceptance of feelings rather than denial, as there is growing evidence that this stress we carry inside of us, if not released, can cause us harm.

The concept of hiding emotions is receding as generations pass on the torch. My parents would not at all have been happy with themselves about crying at work because it showed vulnerability, whereas nowadays, the conventional wisdom and science shows that being open to show feelings fosters connection (read up on works from academic and storyteller Brené

Brown (Ref. 24)). I have been in workshops where people have shed tears while telling a personal story, and the room has been full of genuine warmth and kindness towards them. Yet, there will be others where a sly toxicity lurks; a sensing of someone else's apparent weakness which could be exploited. We still have the 'feeling' that we should have some reservation about showing our feelings and, of course, we don't want to spend all day letting emotions overspill and affect others or our relationships with them.

There is a difference, too, between showing emotions and having them. Sometimes we let them out and regret it afterwards. We do this because when stressed, our rational executive functioning part of the brain (in the PFC) cedes ground to the stressy amygdala. Emotional thoughts win out over calm assuredness. But soon, the PFC recovers control and persuades the amygdala to stand down, so to speak, and then the brain can rationally assess where things have got to. This is where, unfortunately, you might start to feel some remorse over the actions you took or the words you aired. You may wince in memory at that thing you said or when imagining yourself having that tantrum. If you're not careful, you can go round in this loop, and dwell on what happened rather than process it and move on.

In summary, we cannot deny that emotions are part of us. It is healthy to lean in, to experience them, then let them out. This tool is to help with those emotions which you have already experienced and are still struggling with. You can't move on because something is stuck, and you can't let it go.

## Handling emotions, including journalling exercise on ETC

In the workshops we run, there is a module on handling difficult emotions, and I guide the cohorts on a meditation exercise which morphs into a journaling exercise. If you scan the QR code below, you will go to a recording I made of this exercise. This is often very powerful in 1-2-1 sessions where I can tailor the exercise to the client's personal situation.

Everyone is different, and some prefer doing the exercise together (i.e., meditation, then journal), others like doing one or the other. Do whatever works for you. These ideas are not prescriptive and inflexible.

This QR code will take you to my YouTube recording on Handling Difficult Emotions. The ETC exercise is contained within this, but I recommend you playing the whole recording from start to finish and doing the full exercise.

If you don't want to go through the meditation exercise, then you could simply walk through this process. I would do this as a journaling exercise, but of course, you may want to spend a few moments collecting your thoughts before you do it. When doing the journalling, let your writing flow—don't censor or you might bury emotions and lie to yourself.

**When to use this:** After you have been through a 'negative' emotional experience, give yourself some space to reflect. Then, using writing or simply being with your thoughts, follow the process below. Take as long as you like over each of the steps but make sure you get everything out you want to say.

**Emotions**: What were the emotions you were feeling? Anger? Jealousy? Rage? How strong? Be honest with yourself. Where did you feel it in the body? Do you still feel it now?

**Truth**: Now you have some distance, what are the facts as you see them? What's behind your feeling do you think? Is there anything you thought before which isn't true? Can you cut yourself some slack but also learn something?

**Choices**: So, what will you do now? Can you see a path forward? Even if it is to do nothing. At least you can see a new angle and take some learnings.

The key is to recognise that emotions are human but be aware that you have choices moving on from the event. You may feel uncomfortable reliving a difficult experience, but with this method, you will move on quicker.

Sometimes a good metaphor can help us understand a concept. It asks the brain to make connections and form pictures to land an idea. Images are the language of the unconscious. In teaching mindfulness, and in particular the acceptance and processing of difficult thoughts, I like to use 'The Guest House', a poem by the thirteenth century Persian poet Rumi. You will find loads of quotes from him all over social media. He seemed like a wise fellow.

I will let you read the poem and make up your own mind about what it means.

> This being human is a guest house.
> Every morning a new arrival.
>
> A joy, a depression, a meanness,
> some momentary awareness comes
> as an unexpected visitor.
>
> Welcome and entertain them all!
> Even if they're a crowd of sorrows,
> who violently sweep your house
> empty of its furniture,
> still, treat each guest honourably.
> He may be clearing you out
> for some new delight.
>
> The dark thought, the shame, the malice,
> meet them at the door laughing,
> and invite them in.
>
> Be grateful for whoever comes,
> because each has been sent
> as a guide from beyond.

# CHAPTER 10
# RUNG 5: DISENGAGE

I do like some alone time. I love to spend time on the golf course by myself; some people think I am mad (or sad). But for me, it is an opportunity to clear my mind and recharge. I love being with people and connecting with them. I love to socialise, but I do need to get away from that to recharge my batteries, and in some ways, process the interactions I have had with others. This is not what this rung of the ladder is all about, however. This is when social experiences become abhorrent, something to dread or avoid. This is when we are too tired to care what others think about us, and our care for them is on a similar point on the scale. Like a snail retreating into its shell, like a mouse scurrying into a hole, this is where we put up our shutters and lock the world out.

Here, near the precarious top of the ladder now, not only do we lack care for ourselves and others, but we are also feeling pessimistic about the future. Even one or two rungs further down, we may have felt like there was something we could do to make the job better, but now we couldn't care less. Our energy—even to be scathing, sceptical, and have a good old moan—has leaked away, and now we just take everything on the chin and keep going. Our lack of get-up-and-go means our general efficacy has reduced, yet stress levels remain high. We couldn't care about the job, but we do still care about surviving. We are just struggling to put ourselves together to do anything about it. Passion for the job (and life) has all but disappeared, yet we still feel a sense of overwhelm about the amount of work we have to do. We often sit with tears welling up and about to fall as we try and get through another day.

There are a number of parallels with depression here, and sometimes it is hard to discern between the two conditions. It is difficult to get any meaningful data out because there is so much overlap. The key points to mention, however, are that while depression can be a result of a chemical imbalance as well as a possible life event, burnout is due to an overwhelming amount to do or the conditions we are faced with in the workplace (Chapter 3). It is possible, generally speaking, to recover from burnout quicker than depression, but hard to show that definitively since symptoms may overlap. I did read of a useful distinction in the book *Burnout: A Guide to Identifying Burnout and Pathways to Recovery* by Gordon Parker, Gabriella Tavella, and Kerrie Eyers (Ref. 7):

'Burnout feels like helplessness;
Depression feels like hopelessness.'

This made me come to the realisation that with burnout, if we can get help, then we can recover relatively quickly. I don't mean to cast depression sufferers to the wolves and say there is no hope. The statement only says, 'feels like.' It doesn't have to be that way. But with burnout, if we feel helpless, then we can get help, can't we? And that is probably far easier than being able to conjure up hope without any solid justification for it. The only thing is, when we are at this stage, we don't feel like asking for it because that means involving other people and that seems to be the last thing we want to do.

It is understandable that we begin to withdraw from our relationships, or they start to go skewwhiff. In this state of chronic stress, we will be more closed-minded, take comments the wrong way, and be over-defensive when negative feedback is given. If we are not in constant contact with someone, we might start inventing stories as to why this is. They don't like us. They want to keep us out of the loop. Our last email upset them. All this negative imagination will further fuel stress, and so the cycle continues.

## How to re-engage

That's why a book like this can help you. Because if you were left to your own devices, you wouldn't do the things I am asking you to do. We are, as an evolutionary necessity, herd animals. Our success at conquering (at least for the time being) our environment is due in no small part to our ability to cooperate and learn from each other. As part of a hunter-gatherer tribe, if we went it alone, we would not have access to the resources to help us survive. We would be actively picked on and perhaps excommunicated from the group, leaving us lonely and isolated. We need to look out for each other, and as much as you might be suffering, there will be others around you in a different boat but on the same ocean.

Feeling the way you are on the Disengage rung, you could easily pour scorn on the advice to get back in the ring, so to speak. Remember, you actively want to withdraw from social situations, as your confidence is low and you have a lot of personal issues to fix. You think that having some downtime socially will give you that break.

## How social support can ease your pain

Let's for a moment switch gears from the emotional pain we are suffering to physical pain. Over the last few decades, there has been a radical shift in the approach to managing back pain. Previously, it was thought that such discomfort must have a biological cause, whether it is a bulging disc or general spinal injury. Advancements in neuroscience showed the medical community that there was more to pain than just biology. It turns out the brain is very adept at turning up the pain signals in the body when it feels anxious or under threat (perceived or real, remember). This is a psychological factor. There is also a biological factor remaining too, of course, although most doctors and specialists find it very difficult to pinpoint the actual physical problem. There is also a social factor. This is where I draw a parallel, so just bear with me. If we have pain in the body, the natural response is to protect it. Don't move, as it might hurt. This is a normal fight against pain, and a reason why the alarm is sounded—as a warning against doing further damage. But when there is no actual cause, it seems counter-intuitive not to move. What is the body protecting itself against?

In the modern approach, known as the *biopsychosocial* method, a holistic approach to managing the pain is adopted (Ref. 36). A combination of physiotherapy, stress reduction, and social support is the key to recovery. The latter, in the case of back pain, is to approach movement as a necessary part of recovery, rather than avoiding it. Avoidance leads to a tension in the muscles as a subconscious desire to protect the body activates itself. This is counterproductive in most cases, as the tension leads to more muscular problems. It is possible to highlight parallels behind this chronic pain and that of mental burnout. I am not saying that either issue is devoid of causes; far from it. But the avoidance of movement with physical pain (not getting involved in sport, not working, not exercising) is not unlike the avoidance of social engagement we find ourselves experiencing on this rung. The more we can ease ourselves back into social activation, then the more we loosen our mental muscles and get them back to normal.

As I mentioned in the Neglect and Cynicism stages, social connection is vital, and it means we are not alone with our problems. There is a difference between being lonely and being alone. We can appear to have lots of friends and yet be isolated from them. Somehow, I find this the biggest barrier to my personal mental well-being. Our human brains, we have learned, need to try and control the environment they are in. We like to know what's going on around us. Human language was most likely developed so that we could gossip about each other and learn about who was who in the tribe. We needed to know who we could trust in an environment where it was impossible to know everything about everybody. This trait still exists in us today. We combine our general nosiness with a wonderful skill of imagination to conjure up a story about why someone hasn't replied to our text message. There may be an abundance of reasons for this. They are depressed, too busy, trying to ghost us, haven't seen it, meant to reply but couldn't find the words, and so on. Whichever one we choose, it is an assumption based on our own feelings at the time, with a sprinkling of prediction as to what their intentions are. This is another primal gift; the tendency to anticipate others' actions, just in case it is to spring upon us in the night and slit our throats. It keeps us on our toes and makes for an ability to imagine a range of possibilities. Unfortunately for us (or fortunately, as this trait has kept us alive for millennia), this prediction tends towards the negative for obvious reasons. There is a lot we can do with retraining the neural pathways to think along less negative lines, but there is no substitute for reaching out and connecting. When we do meet up with someone in person after a feeling of absence, it is like dipping our feet in a warm bath. Suddenly, we feel comfortable and safe again. We find that our friends are only too happy to listen—the ones who are really our friends, that is.

## Too many friends?

Cliché alert. Those of us with social media accounts may have a multitude of friends or followers. But many of them, you probably don't even know at all! Way back when I was a kid, when computers couldn't really talk to each other and were only for playing *Galaxians*, I did have friends—a close circle of five or six, and then at any one time, someone I would call a best friend. We were joined at the hip and knew each other's foibles inside out. We would stand in those groups at break times and lunchtimes and knock around after school when we got a little older, then inevitably go to the pub together (when over 18 of course …). It was as if we had concentric circles of friends, although I never thought it so clinically at the time. In my very inner circle was my best friend, then in the next one outside of that was that group of six, then in the next one outside of that was my whole class, maybe. Nowadays, it seems the circles are there but just less well defined. In fact, it seems like there is one huge circle, so much so that all of that 'friendship' becomes diluted and unsatisfactory. It feels exhausting keeping up with a big circle of people, trying to stay interested in what they are up to, but with the busyness of life, we only have time to politely scratch the surface. There are too many plates to spin.

And of course, we know it's the same the other way around if we stop to think about it. People aren't getting in touch with us very often because they have too much on and are as overwhelmed as we are by the amount of people to keep in touch with. We could fill our diaries very easily with coffees and get-togethers. But sometimes we don't bother at all, and especially on the Disengage rung of the ladder. The task of getting in touch with people gets too much. Taking it personally if someone doesn't respond only makes our mood worse. If we are feeling okay, then we don't want to exhaust ourselves further by constantly being upbeat with people. This, of course, varies depending on whether you are an introvert or an extrovert. If you don't know which of these two types you are, then just sit down and think—where do I get my energy from? Is it from others or do you inspire it in yourself? If you are the former, you are an extrovert and need others to lift you. You absolutely need a plan to re-engage socially. If you are an introvert, getting inspiration mostly from within, yet your behaviour is different and more withdrawn than normal, then you need to do the same.

## Friends' circles

TIP: If you find yourself daunted by a long list of people you could potentially contact but then don't because it all seems too much, then try this. I got this from a delegate on a workshop who said that she 'rotated' getting in contact with people she knew, simply because it was too overwhelming to keep in touch with all of them. So, make a list of all the people you know and would like to keep in touch with, and then divide them down into different circles-based on frequency of contact. There are those you see every week (inner circle), those you see once a month (middle circle), and those you keep in touch with once a quarter or once a year (outer circle). Does it sound horrendously callous? Not if it means you do keep in touch with people, rather than be so overwhelmed you don't bother with anyone!

The tools in this section are mostly focused on connection, for obvious reasons. In every problem, there is a disguised opportunity. There is no better way to start perhaps than to tear up your friend list and start again with a blank page. Only, the page isn't blank. The first activity in this section is based on a concept from the author in his book *Vital Friends* (Ref. 37). The idea is built upon the premise that there are certain friendship roles which we all need filling to enable our wellbeing, as if we were casting for a play in a theatre company. The definitions of these roles are stated in the table below. The research shows that people who have 'best friends' at work are generally more productive than those who don't, and they are less likely to leave their jobs or the company. This is not just about work, however. We are a holistic entity as a person, so this applies to personal relationships as well as professional ones.

In completing this activity, you can look at each role and write the name of someone you know who fulfils that for you. It doesn't matter whether it is a spouse, friend, family member, co-worker, or boss—just think of someone who occupies that role for you. You may get a blurring between work, friends, and love, but that's okay. If you can't think of anyone, then move on to the next one. Don't think too much and force-fit people into roles. It could be that a friend, for example, does one of those jobs for you and nothing else, that's okay too. Or they may fit into more than one position in the table.

People come in and out of our lives, and we will find that the roles become vacant and need to be filled again. I do realise that sounds clinical, but it's not. It really will enhance a relationship we have with someone. Long-term relationships morph over time—do you ever find that you wonder why you keep in touch with someone, even your best friend? You look at them as times and circumstances change and ask if you still have enough in common. I had a situation where I realised my values and interests seem to have diverged so much from a friend of mine that I started to find their company jarring. We didn't agree on a lot of things, and I am quite prepared to admit my part in the problem. The older I get, the grumpier I get, and the less I can let go of something where I don't see eye to eye with someone. (On reflection, maybe it's me and me alone that has changed, but that's beside the point!) I looked down the table below and realised that they did have a role. He was a mind-opener, someone who would ask me difficult questions and push my understanding a little. He was playing this role passively, teaching me that just by sticking to his guns that there are other opinions which are valid aside from my own, but also actively asking me the difficult questions which got under my skin and forced me to think. This has further cemented our relationship, and we have rediscovered some of our old joy, maybe because I have let go of worrying about it. I told him about this concept of sharing, and he laughed and called me names for not mentioning it sooner.

## Disengage Stage Remedies/Tool 13/ Vital Friends

| Friend Role | Description |
|---|---|
| Builder | Motivator who pushes you to the finish line. They want you to succeed, but never compete with you. |
| Champion | Has your back, sings your praises, even when you are not around. They stand up for you and what you believe in. |
| Collaborator | Relates to your passions and interests. You often have similar ambitions in work and life. Often the basis for a great friendship. |
| Companion | They are there for you through the rough and the smooth. Your bond is virtually unbreakable. They take care of you and provide emotional support. |
| Connector | Builds bridges and introduces you to others. They help you get what you need by connecting you to the right people. |
| Energiser | Gives you a boost when you need it. A fun friend. They pick you up when you are down. |
| Mind-opener | Expands your horizons and encourages you to embrace new ideas. Asks you the right, and sometimes difficult, questions to make you think differently. |
| Navigator | Guides and advises you to keep heading in the right direction. They help you to see a positive future while keeping you grounded. |

(*Vital Friends* from Tom Rath, Ref. 37)

Do try this exercise. At this stage, it just might trigger something important for you and remind you just why we have friends. Pleasant memories may flood back, crowding out the negative ones, which your brain is only too happy to keep showing you at the moment. There may even be tears as you recall just what good times you were having. This is good! Emotional outpouring is the start of recovery—the beginning of climbing the ladder to normality.

Please note. I once had a course where someone basically refused to do the activity, as they felt it was wrong to put labels on people like this and that we can't be put into boxes. Well, fair enough, but we are not really doing that. We are identifying that which we need and reinforcing how important that person is to us. This is only a short exercise that you might do once every six months or so, but if you read the book, you will note that the author encourages people to do the exercise together. Sharing with each other of how you need them enhances the connection. Even if you are alone in completing the exercise, then tell people who occupy those roles what they do for you. It will make them feel good.

Create a blank table for you to have a go yourself. Take approximately 10 minutes to do this.

You may find:

- The same person crops up
- You cannot fulfil all of the roles
- A mixture between work and personal life—partners/family/friends/colleagues

- People come to mind who used to play that role and you have lost touch

There are no wrong answers. This is a thought-provoking exercise to get you thinking about re-engagement. Don't forget it's not all about you. You can play these roles for others too.

## Pay attention

I didn't know just how important it is to pay attention to other people until I learned of this psychological study. We have all experienced the affrontery of trying to talk to someone when they are not present. They glance at a phone while we are speaking to them or hold their hand up as they finish texting, and then say, 'Right, now I am with you,' even if they are not. By then, we might not want to be with *them*.

The issue is that we are all so busy multitasking, striving, and achieving, that we take very little time for others, as well as ourselves. There is always something waiting to be done in our minds, another task to tick off. We might start talking to someone, and then something they say triggers something in our minds. 'Damn I forgot to make that call to so-and-so!' and then our heads are lost to thinking, calculating the consequences of not making that call (storytelling) rather than staying in the present moment. We know from what we have discussed in this book, that the least stressful course of action, at any time, is to focus on one thing at a time, but that it is very difficult to do so. We might not want to listen to every infinite detail of our loved one's day, but we can certainly at least try and make it fun. Just think how much better they will feel after this, being listened to and as if their news counts. We can practice active listening, challenging ourselves as to how many words we can remember, listen to the pitch in their voice, how it rises and falls as their energies shift. Imagine we needed to go and tell this story to someone else. How could we be as accurate as possible in its recounting? What is the real core point of what they have to say? Good old-fashioned active listening skills.

## The first four minutes is all that counts

The twist to this tale is that, although you might be dreading the prospect now of spending an entire evening listening to unexciting yarns, the only part that really counts in the other person's mind is the *first four minutes*. Research shows that subconsciously, the other person only really cares about having your full attention in the first four minutes of the interaction, whether it is a brand-new relationship or an established one. After that, you are sort of free to do your own thing, so if you do find that you are being bored to tears or need to go off to the loo or something, then if you can hang in for roughly the time it takes for an egg to boil, then you are golden. You might draw the line at setting your stopwatch going, then counting them down through the last few seconds of their prime attention time.

We are told when we are very young, when invited to tea at someone's house, that 'first impressions are lasting,' particularly through nonverbal communication. In fact, a jury, apparently, will make up its mind within 7 to 17 seconds about its secret verdict on a defendant before any evidence is presented, simply by the cut of their jib. Cruelly, symmetrical faces get a positive view, and asymmetrical ones are looked upon less so. Once again, we have millions of years of evolution to thank for this. It is in our DNA to spot an aggressive expression fractionally before a friendly one, so quickly that the conscious mind hasn't even had the chance to register either. It is all done in the unconscious and a part of our safety monitoring apparatus within.

So, it's all very quick, and the cliché is a cliché because it is true. First impressions are indeed lasting; be there for four minutes, then you can do what you like, within reason. If you would like to be entertained for slightly more than four minutes, then a link to a YouTube video is included in the references (Ref. 32) where you can see humourist and motivational speaker, Steve McDermott talking on the subject, and how he uses it in his home life.

## Disengage Stage Remedies/Tool 14/ The Four Minute Rule

The instructions are so easy: just read the above and consciously be present when someone is talking to you. Avoid any distraction if you can. Remember it's only for four minutes.

## Lack of control—can't see the wood for the trees

On the Disengage rung, we have focused so far on relationships, for obvious reasons. The tools are intended to give reasons to believe that it is essential to become socially connected again after some unnatural withdrawal in that regard. Note that 'disengagement' also applies to passion for the work we do at this point too. There may be active and deliberate withdrawal from working the hours we were during earlier stages. This might come from within, a feeling of having little left to give or that if our approach is not working, then we should try something different. It might also come from gentle pressure from partners, family and friends.

How do we motivate ourselves to re-engage with our work at this stage, when in actual fact, we are more likely to think about quitting? That may well be the outcome, but it won't always be the right solution. Instead of encouraging a walk-out here, I propose another way to regain motivation in what we do, in life and work, and that is to take back control of it.

Way back on this ladder when we had more fight in us, there was a push to get things done, and we would have spent more time doing rather than complaining. Then, of course, we started talking more about problems, rather than solutions, and ended up in an echo chamber of negativity. We sounded off to our colleagues, and they reflected it back possibly, confirming our self-righteousness. Sometimes of course, they can pull us back from the brink of despair, by offering different perspectives. Now that we are spending more time alone, the inner dialogue is where all of this unhappiness resides, imprisoned in our minds. There's no external influence to snap us out of it, and remember, we are still operating here, having a job to do. We are burning out, not burned out already, so we are still going, even if low on batteries. We have people depending on our support or inputs, but we are overwhelmed because our efficacy is at rock bottom levels.

We are also desperate because we want to have some control back. This is a fundamental human need, to have some control over the environment around us. One of the predictors of burnout is to feel as if we have no agency over the work we do. At this stage, we have lost much control over what we do, mostly because of external influences, but partly due to our own lack of efficacy. Our confidence is low which leads to inaction. This means we have less impact over others and become more reactive than proactive. We go back to complaining-mode time and again, because of frustration at the way things are.

This is when it is time to rip up all of our to-do lists and start again. For this next tool, I can think of no better proponent than Dr. Stephen Covey, who wrote the timeless classic *The Seven Habits of Highly Effective People* (Ref. 26). In his early chapters, he explained a habit called 'First Things First.' The principle is simple but needs some structure to explain it, and to operate within it. What more perfect structure to demonstrate this could there be than a circle?

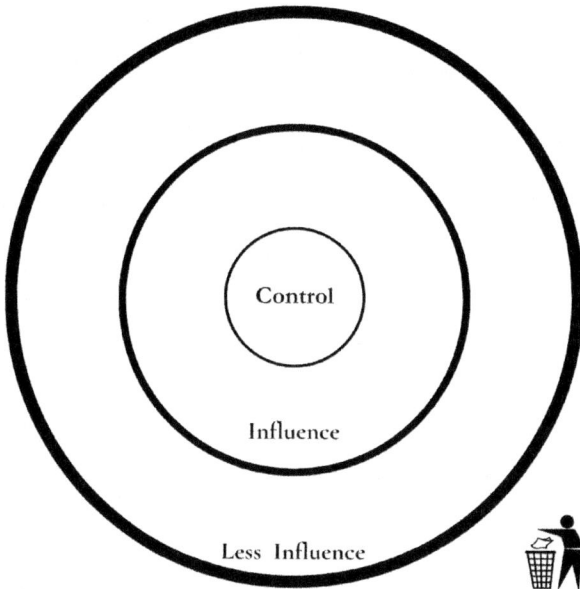

*Figure 7: The Circles of Control*

Covey talked of focusing on our own inner circle of action, working exclusively on what we have power over—what is in our direct control. He called the circles slightly different things, so I won't confuse you by referring to his model any further, only to add that the principle is exactly the same. The circles of Influence and Less Influence you see in the diagram (Figure 7) are where we tackle tasks/projects/concepts only after we have dealt with everything in the Circle of Control. The very first concept within there is our attitude. We can change our mind to how we think about *anything*. No matter where our burnout journey might be taking us, we always have the right to choose how to be.

You then move on to whatever else you have control of. It might be writing an email to your boss suggesting an improvement in the way the department is staffed so that you may avoid burning out. That's in your direct control. You can suggest what you like. You can't control their response; you can only influence it by how you present your idea. So, their reaction or decision goes in the Influence circle. If they need to get somebody else to do something, then that would go in the Less Influence circle, because that is even less in your control.

You can populate the circles with everything else related to this particular project or idea. What starts to happen is three key factors:

1. You focus only on your area of control and gain confidence by working here, because you act rather than procrastinate.

2. You can prepare for anything in the other circles so you can anticipate. In your planning for the re-staffing, you might record a prediction that someone might reject it for some reason, so you can anticipate that.

3. As Dr. Covey noticed—your Circle of Control starts to grow as you become more proactive and realise that you have more agency than you thought, giving you more power.

Then, outside the outer circle is called the Recycling Bin—you can put stuff in here that you have acknowledged you can do literally nothing about and feel a sense of relief and psychological victory as you dump it in here. This, however, is where we tend to spend a lot of rumination time, partly because as humans, don't we love the opportunity to feel righteous indignation? *How can this be happening? They haven't got a clue, have they?* And aren't we always right? Well, this is where the phrase 'It is what it is' becomes very pertinent and practical indeed. I hear it all the time now, and while it might sometimes be an excuse for a shoulder-shrugging resignation and opportunity to sidestep solving a big problem, it is also the most practical way to get *present* with an issue, to move on from where we are *now*, not pointlessly wishing things were, or could have been, different. The phrase already indicates that there is no perfect solution given the constraints you have, thus encouraging a greater quantity of ideas. We tend to go into perpetual whinge status when we do not appear to have control over what we do, but this exercise should prove to you that you have more than it might initially appear. You may not be solving everything here, but you will nudge forward and give yourself some confidence back.

As you become more proactive and act on what you can control, this then increases your power. You are back in command of yourself, making proposals, taking the initiative. This is how your inner circle expands, especially as you are anticipating and resolving issues.

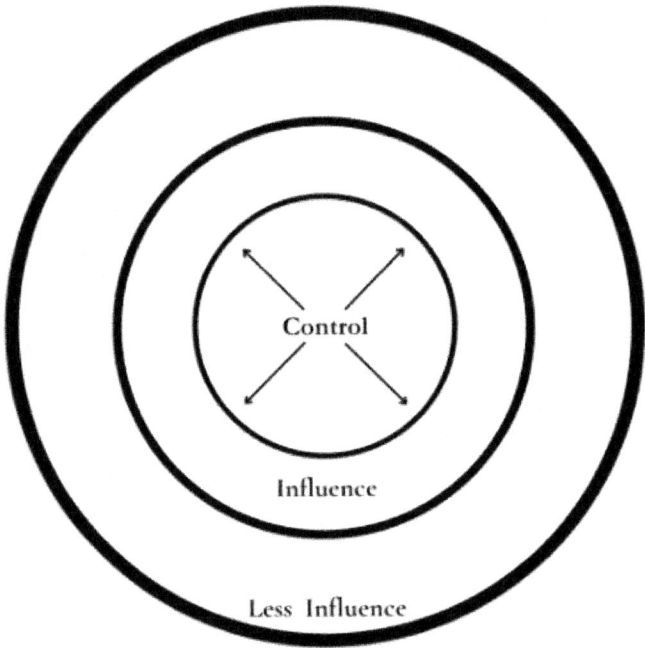

*Figure 8. Expanded Circles of Control*

Giving yourself a greater sense of control will boost your confidence, your sense of reward for what you do, and it might just kick-start a journey back down or off the ladder.

# Disengage Stage Remedies/Tool 15/ Circles of Control

## Circles of control: an example

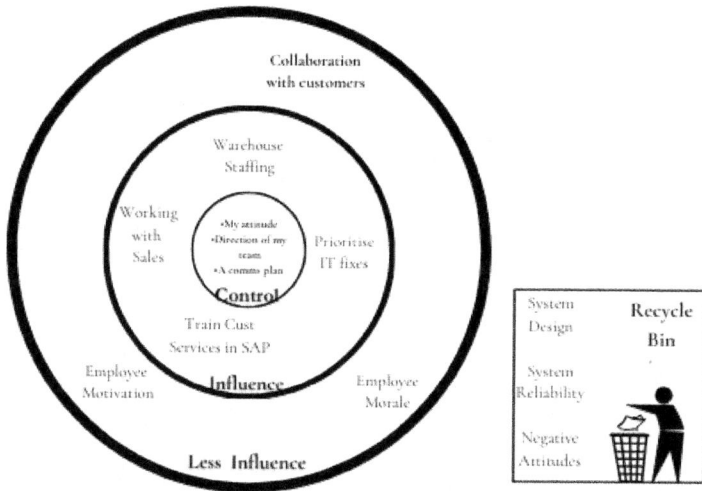

*Figure 9. Circles of Control—my example*

Here is an example of a Circle of Control which helped me get through a difficult time. Here is the context and the thinking.

**Context:** When I was in Canada my boss left a position leaving me as Acting Director. We were just about to go through a major systems transition to a new integrated business platform. It was massive in terms of change, and predictably we had a correspondingly sizeable problem list. We were shipping food to retailers warehouses and stores but we had no idea what was going where—losing orders, losing sales, long hours, little reward. We were going through the mill. Customers, and naturally our sales team too, were screaming blue murder.

As Customer Service Director, my goal was to 'get a grip' on the situation and start to, with the help of my peers, figure out how to use the system so that we knew what was going on. It was also to identify what we needed fixing first, such was the scale of our bug list. We had a 'Command Centre' set up for this, which was one of the best experiences of my career in hindsight. There is nothing like a good crisis to get people focused on an end goal.

My teams were equally unhappy. Long hours, customers bending their ear, no control over what was going on. They were coping with a new system, performing unreliably, and having insufficient quality information for them and their customers. It was all too much, so not surprisingly, a lot of grumbling was taking place.

**Circles of Control:** how did I personally cope with my situation. What could I control and what couldn't I?

**Control:** My attitude—above all else. We are where we are. Let's get on it and fix this. What is the alternative? What can I do? I can direct my team. I can't control their response, but they needed orders, so that's what I gave them. I could also give some idea to our customers of what we were doing and when we expected to have normality resumed, a communications plan. I am always in control of how I send messages out and hopefully influence the receiver's understanding of it.

**Influence:** I could ask for the system fixes I wanted based on what the customers and my team needed, but this was a big organisation with lots of stakeholders. I didn't run the IT team. I worked with the sales teams and warehousing/transport to prioritise what we ship first and to whom. I didn't own the final decision, but I could make recommendations. I could train my teams in using the system, but I could not control their responsiveness.

And so on. Outside of my control, in the Recycling Bin, were things like the system design. I had no influence over that or our software provider. Its reliability was clearly in the lap of the gods too. Same goes for negative attitudes of employees, frankly. In this context all we could do was work through it and hopefully the consequence would be a happier workforce. That was always my aim, but I could do nothing about it directly, other than keep communicating, educating and supporting.

I think it worked. We fixed the problems and moved on eventually after months of knocking over the issues. There was a lot of drama, but we got through. I ended up enjoying the experience when it could have burned me out. The Circles of Control were a big factor in thriving rather than just surviving. My end of year review grade was an Exceeds Expectations rating, when I could have been going off with a breakdown. You can apply this to any project or life situation you are in. Draw three circles on a piece of paper and start to populate them. Don't forget the Recycling Bin. See how your mood starts to change about how much you can control.

# CHAPTER 11
# RUNG 6: EMBERS

The door to burnout is fully open, even if we feel fully closed now. The embers of a fire are the last dying chunks of burning fuel. We are not giving out much heat anymore. In a sense, like a star, we have gone supernova; burning bright, radiating energy in our fight, and then shrinking into the working equivalent of a white dwarf. We have experienced fight-or-flight many times further down the ladder. This is when we have aggression and desire to act. The state or response itself is often referred to with the word 'freeze' tagged on the end, which is what I originally called this chapter. I changed it, as a colleague pointed out that 'freeze' was a bit of a confusing term when talking about burning. Fair point, although a 'freeze' response is what is happening here. Okay ... let's explain what is going on. The freeze response is a very different reaction to danger. When we raise our cortisol levels to give us the weapons to fight or flee, this suggests a visceral and violent action on our part. To freeze, on the other hand, is when all hope is lost, it is the final refuge when fight-or-flight capacity has deserted us. It is nature's kind way of avoiding pain by giving up the fight, such as when a gazelle is overpowered on the savannah by a cheetah. (I really hate talking about this stuff, as I find life so upsetting when it involves the cost to something else's, but it is what it is. That is why there is a food chain, and predators like big cats can't wait around for other things to die before they eat them or they would starve.) The gazelle, having presumably run itself ragged after pumping its system full of cortisol, realises the game is up, so its system goes into shutdown. This will reduce the actual pain that it feels as it is killed by the predator.

In the same way, we have the same ancient system within us which provides a response to safety or danger. An interpretation of this is known as the *polyvagal theory*, as propounded by Stephen Porges in 1994 (Ref. 33). This theory proposes that our autonomic nervous system (ANS) will provide one of three main responses to any given situation where it feels safety or danger. This system predates the brain in our evolution. Simpler organisms than us don't need to analyse the hell out of any given situation, they just need to know if they are in safety or in danger, and then action can be taken accordingly (and quick too), which is why the ANS responds before you even consciously know it. The brain, although lightning fast, is still a bit slow to catch on.

The way it works is via the *vagal nerve*, which is so called because it leaves the brain stem and wanders round the body like a 'vagrant,' connecting to all of the major organs in the body. It keeps the brain in touch with what is going on in our feelings. Recall from the chapter covering emotions (Chapter 9: Rung 4: Cynicism), we feel in the body and we think in our heads, and it is the feeling which ultimately guides our thinking, whether we are aware of it or not. The theory states that there are three main responses for the vagal system, and our behaviours will respond appropriately to them. If you like to keep up to date with wellbeing literature and podcasts, you will hear the term *'vagal tone'* frequently, and in particular how to stimulate the vagus nerve. The purpose of this is to calm the nervous system down so that we can return to rest states in the body. The polyvagal theory covers more complexity than this, and I thought it worth mentioning here as there are correlations between our *'vagal states'* and the journey up The Burnout Ladder®.

Polyvagal theory essentially suggests that our ANS exits in one of three states and can fluctuate between them depending on our perceived level of safety. This is a sense that the body gets, an unconscious evaluation, of the environment and whether it detects safety or danger.

**Ventral Vagal**—When we are open and engaged. Ventral comes from Latin *'vent,'* meaning open. The vagus nerve connects to the front part of the body as well as the back, and this feeling state is when we are front-facing, open to life, engaged, and creative. We would be this way at the bottom of The Burnout Ladder®—ready for anything.

**Sympathetic**—I referred to this earlier, and this is the fight-or-flight response (the sympathetic branch of the ANS). This is mobilisation. This is where we get angry or need to act. This is mid-ladder territory, when we are more emotional, aggressive perhaps, feeling under threat as things get away from us.

**Dorsal Vagal**—When we are closed. You might think of a dorsal fin on a fish. This is when we turn our back on life, closed and alone. We are done. This is the freeze response in nature—playing dead. And sadly, this is where we have got to in burnout. We have nothing left to give.

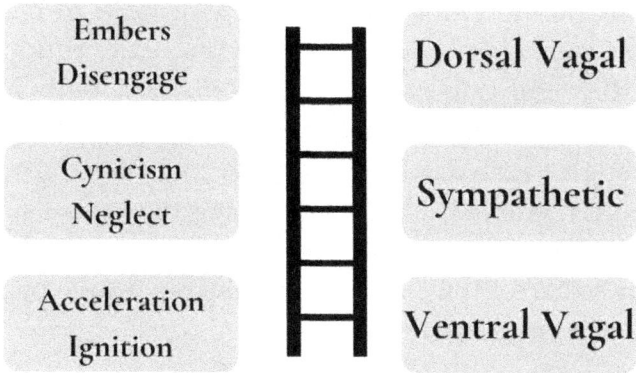

| The Burnout Ladder® | The Polyvagal Ladder |

*Figure 10. The Burnout Ladder® stages vs. the Polyvagal Ladder states*

In polyvagal theory, these system states are presented just like a ladder, funnily enough. If you now imagine Figure 10 shows how the two ladders line up with each other. In Ignition and Acceleration, we are open and collaborative (Ventral Vagal). At Neglect and Cynicism rungs, there is much fight-or-flight and sympathetic (with emotion) behaviour going on. (Sympathetic). There is some mobilisation here, whether it is good or bad behaviour. As we reach Disengage and Embers stages, this corresponds to Dorsal Vagal. It is us turning our back on the world.

In therapy, it is a useful visual to walk through with a client who may be suffering from depression or trauma. To move up the ladder, it is useful to recognize these states and how there is a need to move through them. A person suffering from PTSD who may be experiencing Dorsal Vagal state will need to move through mobilisation phase (Sympathetic) to move up the vagal ladder. I don't see it this way with The Burnout Ladder®. It is simpler than having to move through vagal states of being. We just need to get the hell off our ladder! By adopting the tools I have recommended, when we recognise the stages and the rung we are on, we can merely step off. Sounds easy, but of course, it isn't.

## Is burnout a trauma?

There is Big T Trauma and Little T Trauma. The former is related to significant one-off events (although they may repeat), such as car accidents, assault, abuse, witnessing violence etc., and the latter is still significant but usually longer and more drawn-out. This could be bullying, emotional neglect, divorce, chronic illness, etc. Both have effects on mental health, and it could be argued that burnout is a result of persistent bullying, potentially from the employer, but also self-directed. It is more likely to be Little T Trauma because it is a process in stages rather than single events. Ok, so what does that mean for us

Peter A. Levine, in his book *Waking the Tiger* (Ref. 34), argues that trauma is not just a psychological problem, it is a somatic one too. He goes on to posit that therapists often try to treat the original cause of trauma, even though it has happened and cannot be changed. Instead, we should look at the impact upon us, and he discusses interesting insights into how the body reacts. We store up energy in the body which does not get 'discharged.' He demonstrates an example where a gazelle might get overhauled by a cheetah on the savannah and dragged back to its home. The gazelle's fight-or-flight mechanism has failed to produce a survival response and so, overwhelmed, it went into freeze to reduce the pain and suffering that would have gone with death. In fact, it did not die but went into a state of suspension as it effectively played dead. If the cheetah then leaves it and goes off to do something else, the gazelle can awaken and get itself out of danger. It will go back to its herd as if nothing has happened. But before it does, it literally shakes off the trauma, which is a discharge of stored energy relating to the trauma. He talks about polar bears who have been sedated and then come around who go through a bodily shaking as if they are extremely cold.

Animals, therefore, shake it off—literally—then go back to their lives as if nothing has happened. Whereas our human brains have the capacity to hold on, hide it away, or deny it, resulting in any number of undesired consequential behaviours. Trauma, in whatever form it manifests itself, keeps us locked in the past, even though we live in the present. If you feel this is happening to you, I strongly recommend talking to a qualified therapist.

In other cases, we may not be suffering any trauma as such. We are simply exhausted and out of fuel. Just like an animal though, we are playing dead. We may look sulky or disengaged when we are in the office, and our friends might be worrying about you. I hope they tell you about it if they do. I was playing golf a year or so ago with a very good friend of mine, and he told me how 'everyone' had been worried about me a few years earlier, when it looked like I was having a tough time at work. I looked pale and ill apparently—this is not unusual however, I am a pasty-looking chap, especially in the winter months. I was touched that they had worried about me, but also, I do wish someone had said something. At the time, I was going through a particularly busy period at work, lots of travel and coordinating a major outsourcing project (which I hated), but I just got on with it, like we all do, not without some complaining of course. So if you see it in another, please call it out.

I have already shown you some tips and tricks to help you get off the ladder at any stage, and some of them are quite obvious, it's just that we can't seem to see the solution in front of us until we step outside of ourselves. I have left it up until now to talk about this one because I didn't want you to get distracted and just get up and not read the book, which I know is a low-down and sneaky trick on my part, but there you have it. I wanted you to read through the book as a whole, as I think that in telling the story of how we climb the ladder, we come across not just one coping mechanism. We get to see a whole tool-bag of them. The most important life-affirming tips are contained within this rung. I just didn't tell you that until now.

## Embers Stage Remedies/Tool 16/Talk

### Let's talk it out

My little secret is that the single most helpful intervention that burnout sufferer, according to Gordon Parker again in *Burnout: A Guide to Identifying Burnout and Pathways to Recovery* (Ref. 7), has discovered is to TALK—either to a mental health professional or friends and family. I know it seems an obvious remedy to take, but we are often not in the mood here at the top of this ladder feeling alone. I probably would say this, as I am a hypnotherapist (which involves a great deal of listening to a client as they talk out their troubles), but everyone should have a therapist of some kind. Or a coach, a mentor, or a guide, whatever we want to call it. Someone who can listen and not judge, who can provide safety and compassion, even if they can't provide a solution—that is for the individual to find, often with guidance.

There are many forms of talking therapy available, and it is not for me to tell you which one to take here. If you feel you are burning out, depressed, suffering with your mental health, then the first step is to see your doctor. It is becoming more common for clients with burnout or depressive symptoms to go for Cognitive Behavioural Therapy (CBT). This does not involve hours and hours of psychodynamics, which involves going deep into childhood experiences for example. The practice of CBT contains many tools, one of which is to review recurrent thought patterns and helps rewire the brain so the individual can follow a different neural pathway and think 'better.' It works on the principle that changing your thought patterns will alter emotions and resulting behaviours (we touched upon this remedy back in Chapter 7: Rung 2: Acceleration, Faulty Thinking).

This may be helpful for some, in fact most, and it is prescribed by the National Health Service for many, especially in the realm of stress, anxiety, and depression. I underwent some CBT myself and found some useful nuggets of information to help me. Unfortunately, because of the amount of work I *felt* I had to get through, I chose to only attend two out of six sessions. I made the personal decision that I could not find the time to leave the office and get help. I didn't put it that way at the time, but now I tell clients who say they can't make a therapy or coaching session because of work, that they are de-prioritising their own mental health. The biggest mistake of all. The job is not so important to be worth more than that. And it is our own responsibility to make the time, rather than playing victim because work is too busy.

The range of CBT tools are quite extensive, and they range from challenging the logic of one's thoughts and reframing them, using something like the Faulty Thinking categorisation technique, to Progressive Muscle Relaxation—a method of distracting the mind from its problem by sequentially tensing and then relaxing body parts. This was one technique I learned at my sessions, and it can be very useful to relax the body, and therefore, the mind. Mind and body are in constant communication, and if one of them is relaxed, then the other tends to follow. The tensing of the body followed by the relaxing of it shows you the difference between the two and allows your brain to map what each feels like. We habitually carry tension in our bodies because of stresses. To let the tension out, we need to identify it and then just breathe it out. This method of relaxation can leave the body and mind in a blissful state.

In my other session, I had been explaining to the therapist that a recurring thorn in my own side was my talent at blaming myself for just about everything that went wrong. If someone gave me a piece of work which didn't meet the brief, it was because I had misexplained the brief. If a meeting I chaired wasn't run to the agenda or time, it was always my fault for letting people talk off-piste. The therapist *hummed* and *hah'd*, then produced a Responsibility Pie Chart, which was a circle printed on a piece of paper, like a big round pie. She then asked me for an example of when I had been solely blaming myself for something going wrong. We then identified (within reason, as it was a complex problem) all the other key players and/or departments involved and drew them into the pie as a slice. The size of their individual piece was roughly dictated by their relative importance in the responsibility for outcomes and goals. This was a revelation to me. I felt as if a huge weight had been lifted from my shoulders. I was part of a multi-national organisation, and even in my one department, there were thousands of people involved. Who was I to think that I was the only one responsible for anything going astray in this project? Of course, we all have a part to play, and so I cannot just wash my hands of it all, but this is the purpose of the pie. I have a piece, but so do others. If I had botched the brief, then the other person had a responsibility to say something if it didn't feel right.

It gave me the new perspective that I couldn't fix everything, but I could focus on my own part (much like the Circles of Control), and then hold others accountable for theirs—make sure I did what I needed to, and only ask others to mow their lawn, so to speak, once I had done mine. One small shift in thinking can have massive advantages in terms of our energy, enthusiasm and general mood.

As I said, the various forms of therapy are numerous, and the issues we have as humans are virtually infinite, so I cannot suggest for you, as the reader, what you should do. I went for CBT because my doctor prescribed it, and it was free. I was annoyed with myself, but at peace with it now, for not making the most of it. Even though the world is full of noise and chatter, talk is underrated.

# Embers Stage Remedies/Tool 17/Sleep

## Sleep, baby, sleep

I should also point out that before I went for CBT, I did have a phone chat with a therapist. I recall very vividly, even though this was eight or nine years ago, the realisation that I came to after she played back my words to me. 'So, when you don't sleep, the world seems so black, and when you have slept well, you feel calm and relaxed.' Well, when you put it that way, it sounds so easy. Just make sure I get plenty of sleep, and then all will be well. Except therein lies a cruel twist of irony. Having woken up at 2 a.m.—again—I now have the clarity of thought that if I can just get back to sleep, my mental health tomorrow will be fine, and if I don't, then I will have a terrible day. The more we want something, the harder it is to get it, especially when it comes to peace of mind and sleep. My desperation prevented me from sleeping, and therefore, I used Progressive Muscle Relaxation to distract me, relax me, then get me off to sleep eventually.

Once again, I am not going into the biological necessities of sleep, circadian rhythms, and all of that. I will leave it to the experts. I don't believe you need to know the ins and outs. In fact, maybe it's better you don't know. You might just need to know some top tips to help you sleep better. One of them, of course, is to manage your stress and anxiety, which is largely what this book is about. I must also point out that I would not wait until the Embers stage to start prioritising sleep, but if you have just jumped in at this chapter because you are experiencing these symptoms, then it is a timely reminder.

Do what you can to get more quality sleep, but don't search for a perfect seven to nine hours every night. I am told consistency is as important as quantity, so going to bed and waking up at regular times is in some ways just as important (as long as it's not three to five hours!). I will leave you in the capable hands of Matthew Walker (Ref. 25) on why you should get some sleep. He refers to a number of compelling reasons such as improved cognitive functioning and memory, avoidance of cardiovascular problems and other illnesses, and even the size of a man's testicles!

Matthew Walker on the importance of sleep

## HEAL yourself through sleep

Try this acronym from https://www.mentalhealth.org.uk/ to help you remember the 4 key factors which will help you sleep better.

- **Health**: Physical pain or health problems can prevent quality sleep. If this is affecting you then seek professional help from a GP or health expert.

- **Environment:** Setting up the right environment trains the brain to think of going to bed as a time to sleep. Avoid devices and TV in your bedroom. Make sure the lighting is not bright as this sends a signal that it is daytime, and you should be awake. Being too warm doesn't help either, so have the room at a cooler temperature. Set a standard time for going to bed and waking up as this will form a rhythm which your brain will get used to.

- **Attitude:** Lying awake worrying won't help you sleep. If this is a problem, use some techniques to help you sleep such as Progressive Muscle Relaxation or Mindfulness. If stress persists, see a mental health professional.

- **Lifestyle:** What you do when you are awake affects your sleep. Watch out for caffeine intake after noon. Limit alcohol intake as too much inhibits the necessary phases of sleep. Be sure to have a healthy diet and also remember that exercise is important too.

## Embers Stage Remedies/Tool 18/Play

*'We don't stop playing because we grow old; we grow old because we stop playing.'*
–George Bernard Shaw

I remember my summer of pain while working in Toronto, after my company had gone through its major systems transition and everything went to hell in a handcart. Less than a year after immigrating from the UK, this was a tough time. Friends had come over to see us, excited to live the experience of our new life in our spacious Canadian home, not to mention the wonders of what Ontario had to offer. I was working at least fifteen hours a day Monday to Friday, and Saturdays were taken up too. Sundays, I was just comatose, watching TV and eating 'potato chips,' mouth open in semi-catatonic state. Sure, I was heading for burnout. I had no idea where I was on the ladder, but I know now that I would have been still at Neglect stage. Everything had to move aside to get the work done, but I wasn't yet feeling like I needed to hide from the world or even that my professional efficacy was below par.

I remember one day going down into the basement where we had the Wii games console; all the bobbing heads and legless bodies always provided some amusement. Everyone who came to visit ended up with their own avatar and an evening of drunken bowling or golf down in the basement. (We also had a bar in there, which contributed to the fun and our downfall on those evenings.) On this particular day, I just switched it on and played a joyous game of Frisbee golf on my own, me against the course, and I was in a kind of heaven. Admittedly, my standard of entertainment wasn't very high at that stage, as I had become so accustomed to the endless crises, running around trying to fix things or get people together to fix them, that staring at a wall would have seemed playful.

When we are kids, we play. When we get older, we stop using the word for ourselves. It is as if we have been forced to grow out of it. Play is how we learned about ourselves. What we were capable of mentally and physically; how to play with others, as well as on our own. Whether it is toy soldiers, dressing up a Barbie or Action Man, building LEGO houses and boats (in the old days before each piece was prescribed for you). It is where we learned fairness, patience, the joy of victory, the pain of defeat. It allows us to be creative, use our imagination, and be magnanimous to our playing partners or opponents. Why should we not sharpen these skills as we get older, especially in a world where, sometimes, to 'play' has a dark edge. We are never quite sure if the rules are the same for all the players. I am a bit crazy, I know, but when playing those games of Frisbee golf, I would make up little tournaments in my head, and the challenge was always to beat someone else's avatar. As a kid, I bemused my parents by playing with balloons in our hall, conjuring up games of football and rugby, making crowd noises as if I was breathing on an ornament before polishing it (you will need to do that yourself now to understand what I am talking about), and being the commentator as well as the players. I was never bored on my own. I loved company but could always amuse myself as long as I had a balloon. What a strange child I must have seemed, as I look back on it from here!

So what! My assertion here is that play is important in whatever form it takes. Especially here now, on this rung of the ladder. There is only one more rung and there is nothing left. The ladder is about to burn down and collapse. George Bernard Shaw was right in his aphorism. We are conditioned to take on more responsibility as we get older, rising to a crescendo in middle age and tailing off later, which is when, curiously, the wrinklies start having fun again, some of them becoming ever more mischievous. The tragedy is that we wait so long to give ourselves this freedom. It doesn't have to take all day, even if that would be nice, but taking time out to play, and even using the word itself, I think, is a psychological benefit. My oldest friend from school used to call me up when we were of legal drinking age and say, 'Are you coming out to play?', meaning that we loosen the shackles of a domestic evening and go and have some fun at the pub or wherever we ended up.

## End of chapter note

I do hope that you haven't leapt to this part of the book because this is where you are on the ladder. If you have, however, then hopefully you have picked up a couple of the most powerful fire hoses here. When I read those words—TALK, SLEEP, PLAY—it feels like one of those dream houses in a lifestyle magazine or supplement where they have those words carved in wood and stuck on the wall to remind of some useful values. When I come to think of it, they aren't bad mantras to live a life by, are they? Not least because they don't include WORK, which is how we have got here in the first place.

If we would only talk to our friends and family, or even a coach or mentor. If we could only enough quality sleep, our bodies and minds would remain in good order, all other things being equal. And if we play, we find joy. The rest should look after itself. If you want to add LAUGH and LOVE and put them on your wall, then be my guest.

# CHAPTER 12:
# STEPPING OFF THE LADDER

Finally, here we are. There is no further rung on the ladder. If you feel you are beyond this point then it is time, most definitely, to talk. We love thinking of ourselves as going up ladders. I hope I have conveyed enough, the necessity to be careful about which ones you climb. We all need to move forward in life, and it doesn't have to be upwards—we can learn a lot from going sideways and enjoying varying experiences. By saying that, I realise, of course, that this goes against fundamental human instinct to progress, to go higher, to take responsibility, to realise our potential. In writing this book, I wanted to offer something which recognises basic human desires to move onwards and upwards in life but encourage the self-awareness that gives the opportunity to look out for the danger signals. We can take evasive action from dangerous situations, or we can also meet them head on. In identifying the predictors of burnout, we haven't discussed very much the concept of having fun. We take work too seriously, even when it is a defining factor in our own self-worth. All jobs need to be taken seriously to some degree, or the world would descend into chaos, but we could throttle back if we wanted to. It isn't the job we are overly fussing about; most of the time, it is ourselves. Our egos generally get in the way. If we could loosen up, and stop taking ourselves so seriously, we might find that the ladder doesn't get so hot, and we can ease our way upwards and enjoy the views as we go.

The Burnout Ladder® came out of a realisation that we too often get caught up in sticky situations at work and in life, either because we can't avoid it or we are just not aware enough of what we are doing to ourselves. I hope this book helps you realise that you can throw a red flag marker down at any stage in the journey, and the step off or descent down the ladder can be less painful than you might think.

If only I had trusted myself more, I never would have spent half the night preparing for a townhall which, barely a day later, hardly a single soul could recall. I would have allowed myself to go and do what I do. It was all fine in the end in terms of delivery. I still get lovely notes from people on that team telling me that I did, in fact, inspire them. Was my extra work the secret of my success? No, I think that if I had only allowed myself to give an appropriate portion of myself, then I would have enjoyed it thoroughly, and inspired even more people.

I am using this concept now to help people develop their own resilience to work stress and to coach them into developing a better work/life balance. There are a number of tools in this book, and I wouldn't expect you to use all of them, nor are they all relevant for you. It does depend on your own situation, your position on the ladder, and your preferences for letting off steam. It is becoming a passion in its own right and the most important topic I feel I can help with. I don't know what's happening with the world, but it seems to be tightening its own noose, and the world of work is becoming ever more frantic and lost. The result is poor attention to well-being, despite the corporate tick-box statements and wishy-washy intents. Generally, managers are poorly equipped to deal with their employees' well-being needs, not to mention their own. It's like sending troops into battle with mud-soaked weaponry. No wonder so many come a cropper and end up taking time off with poor mental health.

I hope you keep this book with you, wherever you go. If you look after it, then it will look after you. It is like a fire extinguisher for your own ladder. I have thoroughly enjoyed putting this together. I just hope it hasn't burned me out. I think finally, at the end of all this, I had better take my own assessment just to make sure.

# ACKNOWLEDGEMENTS

In writing and publishing a book, I realised it is not a sole enterprise. There are inspirations, practical help, people who encourage and share their experience. In burnout, we feel alone and isolated, yet it is heartening to think of all those who contribute, knowingly or not. All of the people mentioned below have played their part and kept me company.

I decided to write this work, or at least turn it into something vaguely publishable, in January 2024, while having a coffee with a colleague, Dave Sheridan, who was listening to me pontificate about possibly writing something. With a wave of a hand, he casually said, 'just get it done!' I thought, 'why not?!' and realised soon enough that his suggestion was both massively empowering and a huge understatement!

Writing a book is no mean feat I realise, and even more arduous than I had suspected. Kelly Saward, a fellow mindfulness teacher and author in her own right, has been instrumental in showing me the ropes of self-publishing and encouraging me to persevere. Becky Warrak, as self-publishing coach, has steered me through the murky fog to arrive safely into port.

I didn't realise that it is customary to send out a draft copy of your book to people who will tell you just how unpolished it is, which is vital feedback and a wake-up call. Katy Sheridan and Jen James; thank you for poring over the roughest of manuscripts and giving me your wise counsel. I think I overworked the proofreaders too. To Noel Parnell and Nicola Muskett, my wife, I will buy you fresh highlighter pens. And to Nicola, thank you so much for tireless support, patience, and actually saying you liked my first draft, which delighted me obviously, even as I adjusted for bias...

The seed of the idea for The Burnout Ladder® came from a client, Shannon Toft, an HR professional, who asked me if my company had a programme on burnout, and I willingly said 'yes!' even though we didn't at the time. There's nothing like promising the Earth to get creativity going! Starting out as a half day workshop, this concept has taken on a life of its own and certainly taken over mine. Also, Gary Black, with whom I have developed culture and resilience training programmes which has helped quite a few.

In self-publishing it is important to do your own marketing, since no one else will do it for you. I have had invaluable insights from Alison Evans, who not only designed my business logo a couple of years back, but also told me as I ran my early ideas past her, that 'Freeze' was not a good title for a rung of the ladder which is burning hot! And so, it became 'Embers.' Always good to have a sense check. I have had very good advice too and highly practical help, in how to aim the book at the people who need it, from the excellent Anna White. For the book cover, I was inspired by Michael and Daniel Burleigh, and their brainstormed sketches while we sat in the pub.

This book would not have been written, nor would I have been doing the job I do and love, but for the inspiration of Aston Colley, a yoga teacher, mindfulness coach, and artist, who helped me not only learn to relax my body and mind, but to understand that I could use these skills to help others. I am forever grateful.

And for all the people—not least my mum, who has always encouraged me to write, as well as other family, friends and whoever would listen to me banging on about writing a book—well, perhaps now I might offer some other topic of conversation. I know you have suffered too. There is also Tilly, who sat with me in the early hours, meowing for food and walking over my keyboard while I stared helplessly at the screen.

# Appendix – The Burnout Ladder®
# Symptoms and Watch-Outs by Rung

| Rung | Symptoms | Watch Outs | Recommended Tools |
|------|----------|------------|-------------------|
| Ignition | • Excitement at the path ahead<br>• Trepidation at the path ahead<br>• Anticipation/ nervousness<br>• High energy<br>• Telling your partner/family/ friends about the potential change | • Not following your own values<br>• Rose-tinted spectacles<br>• The need to be perfect<br>• High expectations of self<br>• Unrealistic expectations<br>• Looking for extra cash<br>• Looking for extra kudos<br>• Needing to impress others<br>• Job-scope creep<br>• Worried you will be perceived negatively if you don't step up/forward | • #1 WOOP<br>• #2 Prudent Perfectionism<br>• #3 Wheel of Life |

| Rung | Symptoms | Watch Outs | Recommended Tools |
|------|----------|------------|-------------------|
| Acceleration | • Adrenaline surge as you step up<br>• Enjoyment at extra effort and work<br>• Cancelling social engagements/hobby time<br>• Logging on at weekends<br>• Going to bed later after working late – affecting sleep quality<br>• Perfectionism overdrive – worrying about mistakes<br>• Negativity due to reality bites<br>• Intermittent energy depletions as stress increases | • Working harder and taking more on (obvious? at this stage you have the energy for it; later you probably won't)<br>• Feeling ok about extra hours and work leaking into the evenings/weekend<br>• Focused on others' views of your work: am I being noticed?<br>• Some negativity after initial optimism: reality check?<br>• Feeling weighed down with amount of work | • #4 Faulty Thinking<br>• #5 Nourishers and Depleters<br>• #6 Force of Habits |

| Rung | Symptoms | Watch Outs | Recommended Tools |
|------|----------|------------|-------------------|
| Neglect | • Fatigue – tired, even after 'good' sleep<br>• Irritability<br>• Lack of physical fitness<br>• Pale, drawn<br>• Concentration wavers<br>• Aching limbs<br>• Poor sleep (adrenaline – heart pumping) | • Mind wanders and difficult to concentrate<br>• Letting big moments slip by as you think about work<br>• Escape into comforting activities – gaming, smoking, drinking<br>• Feeling stressed more often than normal | • #7 The Gift of the Present<br>• #8 Accept Yourself<br>• #9 Get Moving |
| Cynicism | • More mistakes<br>• Emotional outbursts & short fuse<br>• Pessimistic<br>• Lacking care and empathy<br>• Complaining rather than solving<br>• Feeling lack of self-worth | • Passion for job decreasing<br>• Find yourself voicing discontent more – echo chamber<br>• Resenting new initiatives because they don't fit your ideals<br>• Feeling hopeless about your role and its purpose<br>• Starting to lack care for others – lacking empathy | • #10 Gratitude<br>• #11 Be Your Biggest Fan<br>• #12 Emotions, Truth, Choices |

| Rung | Symptoms | Watch Outs | Recommended Tools |
|------|----------|------------|-------------------|
| Disen-gage | • Alone time maxed out<br>• Avoiding social contact<br>• Not making time for liked activities<br>• Tired, Irritable<br>• Still stressed, but lacking get-up-and-go | • Lacking care for yourself<br>• Lacking care or empathy with other people<br>• Feeling a sense of pessimism and hopeless-ness<br>• Going through the motions – but efficacy of work has severe-ly reduced<br>• Lacking any pas-sion for work<br>• A sense of over-whelm when you consider how much to do | • #13 Vital Friends<br>• #14 The Four Minute Rule<br>• #15 Circles of Control |

| Rung | Symptoms | Watch Outs | Recommended Tools |
|------|----------|------------|-------------------|
| Embers | • Continued withdrawal from social interactions<br>• No enjoyment in activities<br>• Inaction<br>• Little or no motivation or passion or anything<br>• Sleep poor – consistent early-morning waking<br>• Cognitive Impairment – ability to concentrate minimal/poor memory and concentration<br>• Indifference to stress<br>• Potential; suicidal thoughts (or at least, "who would care if I wasn't here" thoughts) | • Increased emotional thinking and regretting actions and words<br>• That you think there is no way out of this – there is<br>• Not taking action against physical health problems<br>• Thinking that talking to others is pointless | • #16 Talk<br>• #17 Sleep<br>• #18 Play |

# GLOSSARY OF TERMS

**agency** – the ability to choose or take a course of action

**amygdala** – one of two parts of the brain, in either hemisphere, which has a part to play in detecting threat, as well as novelty

**anxiety** – a disorder where the body has experienced an accumulation of stress, resulting in excessive worrying about future outcomes

**ANS (Autonomic Nervous System)** – a branch of the nervous system responsible for processes over which we have little direct control, i.e., breathing rate, heart rate, blood pressure etc.

**Approach and Avoidance** – Approach is moving towards a desired outcome, whereas Avoidance is moving ways from an undesired one

**AXA** – UK-based insurance company

**CBT (Cognitive Behavioural Therapy)** – talking therapy allowing patients/clients to resolve emotional problems by changing the way they think about them

**cortisol** – stress hormone released by the adrenal glands in response to actual or perceived threat

**DMN** – Default Mode Network—group of brain regions that are more active when a person is not focused on a specific task. Associated with self-reflection, mind-wandering, and other internal thoughts

**dopamine** – chemical messenger (neurotransmitter), which plays numerous roles including stimulating reward pathways in the brain, movement, immune functions

**endorphin** – chemical messenger (neurotransmitter) blocking pain when over-exerted, and producing pleasurable feelings, boosting mood

**Fight-or-Flight Response** – reaction via the Sympathetic branch of the ANS to produce a physical response to threat

**hypocortisolism** – condition where the adrenal glands are not producing sufficient cortisol for an effective Fight-or-Flight response. Commonly linked with burnout, Chronic Fatigue Syndrome, Fibromyalgia etc.

**Impostor Syndrome** – a condition (not medical or a

disorder) where the sufferer experiences anxiety that they have not earned their current position and will be discovered at any time

**Inner critic** – a sense that a person has a part of our personality which overly criticises themselves. Sometimes, misleadingly known as an inner 'voice'

**limbic brain/system** – a series of interconnected brain structures playing a role in emotions, reward, and memory

**Mental Contrasting** – a technique of goal-setting combining forward visualisation with realistic assessment of obstacles. The WOOP process is an example of this

**neurons** – nerve cells which transmit messages through the brain and the body via electrical signals. Approximately 86 billion in one person, mostly in the brain

**neuroplasticity** – the ability to adapt neural pathways in the brain to improve at or take on new tasks via repetition and practice

**oxytocin** – feel good hormone produced as a result of close interaction with another person

**PFC (Pre-Frontal Cortex)** – brain structure responsible for self-regulation and emotional control

**psychoanalysis** – based on theory propounded by Sigmund Freud that problems reside in the subconscious. A theory designed to bring unresolved unconscious conflicts to the surface

**serotonin** – chemical messenger (neurotransmitter) playing a part in mood, appetite, sleep

**stress** – bodily response to demands placed upon the organism. Although stress is seen as a mental issue, it is carried within the body resulting in the hormonal reaction fight-or-flight

**synapses** – junctions between neurons where messages are passed. They are tiny gaps across which the charge is carried

# REFERENCES

1.  'Poor mental health costs UK employers £51 billion a year for employees', Deloitte, https://www.deloitte.com/uk/en/about/press-room/poor-mental-health-costs-uk-employers-51-billion-a-year-for-employees.html
2.  'QD85 Burnout', ICD-11 for Mortality and Morbidity Statistics, International Classification of Diseases, WHO, https://icd.who.int/browse/2024-01/mms/en#129180281
3.  Diagnostic and Statistical Manual of Mental Disorders, American Psychiatric Association, https://www.psychiatry.org/psychiatrists/practice/dsm
4.  Google Trend Search "burnout", https://trends.google.com/trends/explore?date=today%205-y&geo=GB&q=burnout&hl=en
5.  Fyodor Dostoevsky, *The Brothers Karamazov*, ISBN 9789352763344, 9352763343
6.  Herbert Freudenberger, *Burnout: The High Cost of High Achievement*, 1980, ISBN 9780385156646, 0385156642

7. 'Burn-out an "occupational phenomenon": International Classification of Diseases' (classification of burnout as a syndrome, not a medical condition), WHO, https://www.who.int/news/item/28-05-2019-burn-out-an-occupational-phenomenon-international-classification-of-diseases

8. Gordon Parker, Gabriela Tavella, and Kerrie Eyers, *Burnout: A Guide to identifying burnout and pathways to recovery*, ISBN-13: 9781761062148 , ISBN-10: 176106214X

9. Gabriela Tavella and Gordon Parker, 'We're all exhausted but are you experiencing burnout? Here's what to look out for', Sydney Burnout Studies – UNSW, 2021, https://www.unsw.edu.au/newsroom/news/2021/08/we-re-all-exhausted-but-are-you-experiencing-burnout--here-s-wha

10. Maslow's Hierarchy of Needs, https://www.researchhistory.org/2012/06/16/maslows-hierarchy-of-needs/

11. 'Mind health report', AXA, March 2024, p. 16, https://www.axaglobalhealthcare.com/en/wellbeing/emotional/mind-health-report/

12. 'State of the Global Workplace: 2024 Report' Gallup, https://www.gallup.com/workplace/insights.aspx

13. 'The Manager Resilience Report', The Wellbeing Project, https://info.thewellbeingproject.co.uk/manager-resilience-report-2024-download

14. Dr. Christina Maslach, 'Understanding Job Burnout', https://youtu.be/SVlL9Tn-vphA?si=f-sf2f8-E1IFl9KI

15. 'Average earnings by age and region', House of Commons Library, https://common-slibrary.parliament.uk/research-briefings/cbp-8456/#:~:text=Trend%20in%20average%20earnings,1997%2C%20adjusting%20for%20CPI%20inflation

16. 'Flow Theory', Science Direct, Mihaly Csikszentmihalyi's 1990 theory, https://www.science-direct.com/topics/psychology/flow-theory

17. Rick Hanson, *Resilient*, 2018, https://rickhanson.com/

18. Gabrielle Oettingen, WOOP, https://youtu.be/yBaVSJ6zq4c?si=-ZY90rlJVA9pZ-Lv

19. Jennifer Kemp, *The ACT Workbook for Perfectionism*, 2022, ISBN-13: 978-1684038077, ISBN-10:1684038073

20. Kristin Neff, 'The Space Between Self-Esteem and Self Compassion, TEDx Talk, https://youtu.be/IvtZBUSplr4?si=zi2etCfRw7OhOtJG

21. Mark Williams and Daniel Penman, *Mindfulness: A Practical Guide to Finding Peace in a Frantic World*, p.3, ISBN:9780749953089, 074995308X

22. Adrian Chiles, *Winter Walks*, BBC Four, Dec 2023

23. Random Acts of Kindness Foundation, https://www.randomactsofkindness.org/

24. Brene Brown, 'The Power of Vulnerability',

TED Talk, https://youtu.be/iCvmsMzl-F7o?si=aoD637SPdpc4Gg5b

25. Matthew Walker, 'Sleep Is Your Superpower', TED Talk, https://youtu.be/5MuIMqhT8D-M?si=aMXKXrDXV1XxJku9

26. Stephen R Covey, *The 7 Habits of Highly Effective People*, ISBN: 978-1-4711-9520-4

27. Google Oxford Languages: Definition of Neglect

28. Victor Frankl, *Man's Search for Meaning*, ISBN:9781448177684, 1448177685

29. Vidyamala Burch and Daniel Penman, *Mindfulness for Health*, ISBN 978-0749959241, 9780749959241

30. Personality Attributes, Google Gemini

31. Leonard Mlodinow, *Emotional*, ISBN 978-0-141-99039-2

32. Steve McDermott, 'The Four-Minute Rule', https://youtu.be/hiTehy2tjAU?si=OYQzNi-FlQ6aMEcn8

33. Dr Stephen Porges, Polyvagal theory 1994, *The Polyvagal Theory: Neurophysiological Foundations of Emotions, Attachment, Communication, and Self-regulation*, ISBN:9780393709063, 039370906X

34. Peter A. Levine, *Waking the Tiger*, ISBN:9781556432330, 155643233X

35. Bessel van der Kolk, *The Body Keeps The Score*, ISBN:9780141978628, 0141978627

36. David Rogers and Grahame Brown, *Back to Life: How to Unlock Your Pathway to Recovery*

*(When Back Pain Persists)*, ISBN 9781473529601, 1473529603

37. Tom Rath, *Vital Friends: the People You Can't Afford To Live Without*, ISBN: 9781595620071, 1595620079

38. James Clear, *Atomic Habits*, ASIN: B07J1X-QSNK

## About the Author

My name is Alan Muskett, and this is the first book I have ever published. It has always been something of a personal ambition, and I never thought I would do it, but here I am about to press the button to upload the final proof. This book came from a desire to help others avoid the horrendous pitfalls of burning out, which are soul-sucking, and can make us feel that life is not worth living. Ironically, I have almost succumbed to them myself in getting this book finished, and I have had to temper my own insecurities which lead to perfectionism. Thankfully, I have some useful tips here to prevent that relentless climb up The Burnout Ladder®.

I hope the information I provide, and the tools in this book, will give the reader some highly useful tips into turning potential burnout into enjoyment of life once again.

## Work With Me

The book may be the start for you, a thought-provoking epiphany that life doesn't have to be the relentless grind we seem to settle for. If you feel you are struggling with burnout and can't seem to get off the ladder, then I am here to help you.

I work with individuals and teams to help them build good habits and avoid climbing, and re-climbing, The Burnout Ladder®. We can be ambitious, if that is our desire, and still enjoy life.

Here are my details. Get in contact, if you would like to consider working with me in coaching programmes, assessments, or group-work, my social media details are below.

This could be the start of a healthier work/life balance road for you. Check out what services I provide.

**Websites:** www.theburnoutladder.com
www.rightmindfulness.co.uk
**LinkedIn:** www.linkedin.com/in/alan-muskett
-5982296
**Facebook:** https://www.facebook.com/Inkberrow
RightMindfulness
**Instagram:** https://www.instagram.com/alan_
rightmindfulness/

# RECOMMENDED READING

*Atomic Habits: Tiny Changes, Remarkable Results*, James Clear (2018)

*The Body Keeps the Score: Brain, Mind, and Body in the Healing of Trauma*, Bessel Van Der Kolk (2015)

*The Brain: The Story of You*, David Eagleman (2016)

*The Chimp Paradox*, Prof. Steve Peters (2012)

*Emotional, The New Thinking About Feelings*, Leonard Mlodinow (2023)

*Golf is Not a Game of Perfect*, Dr. Bob Rotella (2004)

*Grit: Why Passion and Resilience are the Secrets to Success*, Angela Duckworth (2017)

*Ikigai: The Japanese Secret to a Long and Happy Life*, Héctor Garcia & Francesc Miralles (2017)

*The Kindness of Strangers: Travel Stories that Make your Heart Grow*, Fearghal O'Nuallain (2019)

*Leaders Eat Last*, Simon Sinek (2014)

*A Mindfulness Guide for the Frazzled*, Ruby Wax (2016)

*The Mind Illuminated*, John Yates Ph.D., Matthew Immergut, Jeremy Graves (2017)

*Mindfulness: Finding Peace in a Frantic World*, Mark Williams and Daniel Penman (2011)

*Mindfulness for Health: A Practical Guide to Relieving Pain, Reducing Stress and Restoring Wellbeing*, Vidyamala. Burch and Daniel Penman (2013)

*The Myth of Normal: Trauma, Illness & Healing in a Toxic Culture*, Gabor Maté, Daniel Maté (2022)

*The Obstacle is the Way: The Timeless Art of Turning Trials Into Triumph*, Ryan Holiday (2014)

*The Power of Your Subconscious Mind*, Dr. Joseph Murphy (2019)

*Psycho-Logical: Why Mental Health Goes Wrong, and How to Make Sense of it*, Dean Burnett (2019)

*Resilient: Find Your Inner Strength*, Dr. Richard Hanson (2020)

*The Science of Storytelling: Why Stories Make Us Human, and How to Tell Them Better*, Will Storr (2019)

*The Seven Habits of Highly Effective People*, Stephen R. Covey (1989)

*Surrounded by Idiots: The Four Types of Human Behaviour*, Thomas Erikson (2019)

*Waking the Tiger: Healing Trauma*, Peter A. Levine (1997)

*Wherever You Go, There You Are*, Jon Kabat-Zinn (1994)

*Who Moved My Cheese*, Dr. Spencer Johnson (1998)

*Why Has Nobody Told Me This Before*, Dr. Julie Smith (2022)

Printed in Dunstable, United Kingdom